Strategic Planning Made Easy™

A Practical Guide to Growth and Profitability

Howard W. Olsen, Ph.D. and Nancy D. Olsen

Strategic Planning Made Easy ™
A Practical Guide to Growth and Profitability

Published by
M3 Planning, Inc.
P.O. Box 8021
Reno, NV 89507
Copyright © 2004 M3 Planning, Inc. All rights reserved.

ISBN: 978-0-9748343-2-0
Printing 2004, 2006, 2007, 2011, 2016

Printed in the United States of America

Arrangements for special publication and reduced rates for bulk orders are available from M3 Planning.

Patent Pending

This book is designed to stand alone or to be used as a reference guide in conjunction with the online, interactive "Strategic Plan" located at www.onstrategyhq.com.

Important Note: How to Use This Book

This book is designed to be used as a reference guide in conjunction with the online, interactive "Strategic Plan" located at **www.onstrategyhq.com.** For each step in your Strategic Plan, you will find supporting worksheets. Use the worksheets to develop your thoughts for each respective step.

 Each step and associated worksheet corresponds directly with the online Plan. The online version is recommended as it as allows for dynamic processing of your thoughts and ideas. When you are ready, log on to your Plan and input your thoughts into the online, interactive Strategic Plan. The plan allows you to:
- Integrate each step so that you may develop a cohesive plan,
- Make changes with ease,
- Track your progress,
- Manage your plan throughout the year, and
- Print a complete plan.

About the Authors

Howard W. Olsen, Ph.D., CPA
Dr. Howard Olsen is the President of M3 Planning, Inc. a business development firm. Howard is an entrepreneur with more than 25 years of business experience. He holds a Ph.D. in marketing with an international emphasis and is a CPA. Howard has had years of consulting experience working with clients in the areas of strategic planning, marketing, and financial management. Additionally, he served as an assistant professor of marketing at the University of Nevada, Reno. Howard's desire is to equip leaders with practical tools for organization effectiveness.

Nancy D. Olsen
Nancy Olsen is the Vice President of M3 Planning, Inc., a business development firm that specializes in helping organizations develop their strategy to accomplish their growth plans. She works with clients in developing strategic plans for their organization through an online planning system, consulting, and facilitations. Nancy holds an MS in Education, an MA in Theology, and an MBA in Management. Her expertise is much more than academic, however, as the owner of five small businesses and an entrepreneurial consulting practice. Nancy's desire is to equip organizations to strategically use their resources to impact their communities.

About Us

M3 Planning, founded in 2000, is a strategic planning firm that works with growth-oriented organizations to develop and execute their strategies. Our products and service help organizations save time, get focused, and obtain better results. Our strategy framework is market-focused, balanced scorecard based and research driven. Through years of experience we have uniquely developed an online Strategic Planning System, which has a patent –pending status.

M3 Planning has become a leader in strategic planning services for organizations. Why? Perhaps it's because we deliver integrated, industry-specific planning services for organizations of all sizes. Or maybe it's because we take the mystery out of strategic planning. Or it could be because our services focus as much on the strategy as on the implementation. Or maybe it's because of our 100% dedication to the success of our customers and their growth.

In fact, M3 Planning clients gain more focus, buy-in from their teams, a better use of resources, more time (for work and play), increased employee enthusiasm, and a 12% increase in resource utilization. We are proud to be contributing to the success of organizations of all sizes, in all industries, around the globe. Every organization, no matter the size or resources, wants to be more strategic. We accomplish this in four ways:

- **Strategic Planning System**: <u>OnStrategy</u> is a web-based application for plan development and performance management.
- **Assessments**: We offer several assessments to help organizations determine their strategic position.
- **Strategic Plan Review**: Our virtual strategy team reviews plans to help organizations develop a successful strategy.
- **Books**: We are the authors of *Strategic Planning for Dummies* and the *Strategic Planning Made Easy*™ series.
- **Facilitation**: Our highly experienced strategy experts offer on-site strategic planning sessions for those looking for outside facilitators.
- **Market Research Consulting**: Our Ph.D. level research helps organizations determine what the market wants and uses this data to drive strategic decisions.

TABLE OF CONTENTS

Introduction

Why Do Strategic Planning?

Do you know where your company is going? What will your business be like in three years? Will you be a few steps closer to realizing your vision? No one can predict the future. But if you don't change anything, will the future be any different than the past? Probably not. But one sure-fire way to impact your company's future is to dust off an old tool – the Strategic Plan.

A strategic plan is the "game plan" that a company utilizes to build commitment and to agree on priorities that are essential to its mission and responsive to a dynamic operating environment. Strategic planning is a management tool that can help a company focus, so that all organizational resources are optimally utilized in accomplishing its mission. A strategic plan can help a company position itself in its chosen market, serve constituents, satisfy stakeholders, and achieve successful performance.

Most businesses have a myriad of excuses for not having a formal strategic plan. Excuses have been heard that range from "We're too new," "We're not big enough," to "We've never had one, why start now?" If these excuses sound familiar, here are a few interesting facts: Studies indicate that 50 percent of new businesses fail within the first 18 months due to a lack of direction and approximately 90 percent of all businesses lack a strategic plan. If you are part of the 90 percent, ask yourself: Could your company be more focused? Could you be more effective? Could your staff be more efficient? And most of all, could your company be more successful? Most of us would probably answer "yes" to all of the above. Be part of the 10% with a business that excels - develop a strategic plan.

Strategic planning is a process that helps you focus on understanding your marketplace and on aligning your resources to take advantage of the opportunities in your market. It is a method for setting specific goals and determining a set of actions to achieve those goals and to access the results. A strategic plan drives your business and should be integrated into every fiber of the company, so everyone is helping to move the company in the same direction.

Keep in mind that a strategic plan is a living, dynamic document. Strategic planning is a process that is ongoing and never-ending, changing as the needs in your environment changes. Your plan does not have to be perfect or 100 percent complete to begin implementing it. A rough draft is better than no plan at all. When your company has a clear plan and takes appropriate action, you get "traction" to take you from where you are, to where you want to go! So let's get started!

Group Facilitation

The majority of strategic plans are developed in a team or group setting. Whether you are an outside facilitator or an internal team leader, this book will help you keep the strategic planning session productive and successful. Please see our website www.onstrategyhq.com for additional information about strategic planning facilitation.

Market-Focused Strategic Planning

M3 PLANNING PROCESS

Just what is market-focus strategic planning? To explain this, we first must start with a few definitions:

- *Market Focus* – understanding your customers' needs and wants better than your competitors do and providing your customers with superior products or services.
- *Strategic* – decisions and activities that enable a business to achieve and sustain a competitive advantage and to improve its performance. Businesses that create and sustain a profitable strategy link their internal capabilities (what it does well) and its external industry environment (what the market demands and what competitors offer).
- *Market-Focused Strategic Planning* – the matching of skills and abilities of a company with opportunities in the marketplace to gain a competitive advantage.

The M3 Planning system is a market-focused strategic planning process. The three main concepts that are key to our system are: Mission, Market and Measurement. It is the synergy of these elements implemented through a Market-Focused Strategic Plan that will improve your company's financial performance.

Developing your Mission

Your mission defines your company's purpose and direction based on your company's competitive advantage. A competitive advantage is what makes your company unique. The singular purpose of a strategic plan is to create a sustainable competitive advantage. Fully realized, you will see the bottom-line and organizational effects of having grasped your competitive advantage. You will go through the following steps in "Developing your Mission":

- **Step 1 – Competitive Advantage:** The result of a well-planned and executed strategic plan is to develop a sustainable competitive advantage.
- **Step 2 - Mission Statement:** To define the company's purpose and direction.
- **Step 3 - Vision Statement:** To formulate a picture of what the company's future business makeup will be and where the organization is headed.
- **Step 4 - Core Values:** To identify the authentic core values and beliefs that your company is truly committed to.
- **Step 5 – Strategic Objectives:** To convert the mission and vision into tangible actions, by moving from motive to action. Objectives are long-term, broad, non-measurable, and continuous. Objectives are categorized into four areas – Financial, Customer, Internal/Operational and People/Learning.
- **Step 6 - Internal and External Assessment:** To assess the particular strengths, weaknesses, opportunities, and threats that are strategically important to your company.

Reaching your Market

Your Strategic Plan will focus on your company's unique market. A company can have great people, efficient operations, a good customer base and be successful. If you want to move your company from being average to impactful, you need to understand your customers' needs and wants better than your competitors do. And with that information, provide your customers with superior products or services. To do this you need to: 1) *Gather* information about your customers and your marketplace; 2) *Communicate* the information collected to your managers and employees; and 3) *Respond* to the market's needs by acting on what you learned. Your Strategic Plan will be focused on your market by imbedding these gathering, communicating, and responding activities into your company. You will go through the following steps in "Reaching your Market":

- **Step 7 - Customer Groups:** To identify groups of customers that have similar characteristics and choosing groups to focus on.
- **Step 8 - Value Creating Strategy:** To establish a strategy that matches your company's strengths with market opportunities to position your company in the mind of the customer.
- **Step 9 – Short-Term Goals:** To set goals that converts the long-term objectives into specific performance targets. Effective goals clearly state what, when, how, who and are specifically measurable.

Establishing your Measurement

To help measure and manage your Strategic Plan, we have used the concepts from two Harvard professors and consultants – Kaplan and Norton. The Strategic Scorecard is to be used as both a measurement and management tool to implement your company's strategic plan. Think of it as an instrument panel guiding your company toward achieving an integrated single strategy. The Strategic Scorecard is integrated into every step of your plan. You will go through the following steps in "Establishing your Measurement":

- **Step 10 – Action Items:** To set specific actions/action plans that lead to implementing your goals.
- **Step 11 - Financial Assessment:** To assess the financial viability of your plan. Prioritize key goals and tactics.
- **Step 12 - Strategic Scorecard:** To measure and manage your Strategic Plan.
- **Ongoing - Implementation:** To identify issues that surround who will own the plan; how the plan will be communicated; how the plan will be supported.

KEY TO IMPLEMENTING THE M3 PLANNING PROCESS

Before you start, it is important to know how the plan will be implemented. Consider addressing the following:

- Are you and top leadership committed to implementing a plan to move your company forward?
- What are the names of the key people who need to buy into the plan?
- Are you willing to question the status quo, look at new ways of doing things, ask hard questions, and make decision that are best for customers?
- How will you communicate the plan throughout the company?
- Will you commit money, resources, and time to support the plan?

THE COMPLETED STRATEGIC PLAN

The Strategic Plan creates opportunities for top management and staff to think strategically. It serves as a lever for building commitment and a tool to challenge the organization to stretch itself and improve overall organizational performance.

On the following page you will find the Strategic Plan Map. A full-size map is located at the end of the book. This map serves both as an illustration to guide you through the process and an example of what you can expect when you have completed your plan. You can see how each step in the process works together, in an integrated, holistic manner. Please use this as a reference as you work through each step of the planning process.

Happy Planning!

Strategic Plan Map

5

BE THE BEST.

Aspire to be the best.
Successful companies *deliberately* make choices to be unique and different in everything they do.

Dominate your market
product category
service offering
customer service.

Don't settle for second best.
Create a sustainable competitive advantage.

Competitive Advantage

PURPOSE: The result of a well-planned and executed strategic plan is the development of a sustainable competitive advantage.

Competitive strategy is about being different. It means deliberately choosing to perform activities differently or to perform different activities than rivals to deliver a unique mix of value. -- Michael Porter

Just what is a sustainable competitive advantage? It is simply the answer to: What is your company best at? Your competitive advantage is what your company does better than anyone else. It is something you do that is unique. The sustainable part refers to your ability to continue to do those unique activities over a long time.

Your competitive advantage(s) is the foundation, the cornerstone of your strategic plan. Other elements of your plan tend to morph. But what makes your company unique, your competitive advantages, will stay constant. Throughout the planning process you will need to evaluate every part of your plan to determine whether it supports or detracts from your competitive advantage. For example you will develop goals that make your competitive advantage sustainable and measures that monitor your competitive advantage.

Your competitive advantages, once you have identified them, should endure and grow stronger. The leading organizations in this world have a razor sharp understanding of their competitive advantage. Everything they do builds and nurtures their competitive advantages.

QUESTIONS TO ANSWER:
To uncover your competitive advantages look at your unique strengths. Then look at these unique strengths in comparison to your competitors. Core competencies are unique strengths that stand up against the competition. In the process you discover what draws customers to buy the product or service from you instead of the competition. Answer the following questions on the worksheet provided on the next page.

Unique Strengths – What you do well
Use the convergence of Passion, Purpose, Profit Engine and Resource areas to develop a list of unique strengths. These should be unique – not a laundry list of capabilities, people and resources.

Passion:
- What motivates you to do your business?
- What are you and your people to be deeply passionate about?

Purpose:
- What business are you really in?
- Why does your business exist?

Resource:
- What unique skills, resources, capabilities, and assets set your company apart in the marketplace?
- How are these skills and resources currently used to create value?

Profit Engine:
- What is your primary revenue driver? How do you make money?
  (i.e. profit per customers, profit per customer visits, profit per employee, profit per order, profit per region, profit per billable hour, profit per affiliate, profit per product or service line)

ACTION ITEMS
Write your competitive advantages based on your unique strengths and core competencies.

MARKET FOCUS
A market-focused company understands how it provides unique value to its customers.

Core Competencies – What you do better than your competitors

A core competency is a competitively superior unique strength that the company performs well in comparison to its competitors. It becomes the basis for a company to build its competitive advantage.

List what your company does better in comparison to its competitors on the worksheet provided.

EXAMPLES:

Here are examples from company's who answered the questions "What is my company best at?"

Financial services firm	▪ Ranked in top 10 percent of money managers who beat S&P nationally ▪ Fastest-growing American Funds money manager in '00, '01, & '02 ▪ Only firm ever featured by American Funds in its advisory newsletter
Interior design firm	▪ Increasing developers' sales ratio by 35 percent. ▪ Only design team chosen by the top 10 luxury developers in the state.
Clothing manufacturer	▪ Wearable clothing because "Our clothes fly off the racks."
Emergency service division in county in WA	▪ Providing disaster management, response and recovery efforts for all agencies within its' service territory because of its skilled people and emergency response equipment.
Pershing General Hospital	▪ Provides the one-and-only, high-quality emergency, primary care, and retail pharmacy within its service area ▪ Staffs the hospital with personnel that have superior knowledge to support efficient operations. ▪ Offers the best care possible by maintaining its full staff of highly-experienced nurses.
Surfrider Foundation	▪ Defined focus on environmental issues that relate to the ocean and only the ocean. ▪ Committed people who are extremely passionate about protecting the ocean. ▪ Dedicated to maintaining a bipartisanship view to foster broad-based support.
Abbott	▪ Creating a product portfolio that lowers the cost of health care.
Fannie Mae	▪ Could become the best capital markets player in anything that pertains to mortgages.
Gillette	▪ Could become the best at building global brands of daily necessities that require sophisticated manufacturing technology.
Wells Fargo	▪ Could become the best at running a bank focused on the western United States.

Source: *Good-to-Great* Study that found that the last four companies generated cumulative stock returns that beat the general stock market by an average of seven times in 15 years.

Worksheet: Identifying Your Competitive Advantage

Directions: Based on your answers, map your company's competitive advantage using the guiding definitions below.

Unique Strengths

What you do well?

Unique skills, resources, capabilities, and assets you have in your company.

Directions: Use the convergence of Passion, Purpose, Profit Engine and Resource area to develop a list of strengths. What are your unique strengths?

Examples: People, Knowledge/Expertise Processes, Products, Services, Contracts Brand, Relationships, Intellectual, Property

Your Unique Strengths:

Core Competencies

What you do better than your competitors?

It is a competitively superior company resource that the company performs well in comparison to its competitors.

Directions: Compare your strengths to your competitors. What do you do better than your competitors?

Examples: Consistency, Longevity/Brand development, Depth of knowledge based on experience, Development of the strength Continued innovation & improvement Invest in the strength

Your Core Competencies:

Competitive Advantages

What you do best?

It arises from leveraging a firm's unique skills/ core competencies to implement value-creating strategy that competitors cannot implement as effectively.

Directions: Take your core competencies and match them up with the market need. What needs exist in the market that your competency meets and provides value?

Examples: Market need, Market demand, Client referrals, Word of mouth. Growth Superior performance

Your Competitive Advantages:

Nurtured

Leveraged

11

COMPETITIVE ADVANTAGE

Based on your company's unique strengths and core competencies, write down your company's current or potential competitive advantages? (List 3-5)

EVALUATING IF YOUR COMPETITIVE ADVANTAGE IS SUSTAINABLE

How do you know *when* you have developed a sustainable competitive advantage? Here are three criteria that can help evaluate if you are on the right track and assist in keeping you there:

- Customers must see a **consistent difference** between your product/service and those of your competitors. This difference needs to be obvious to your customers and it must influence their purchasing decision. Example: Coke vs. Pepsi.
- Your competitive advantage must be **difficult to imitate**. Avoid thinking that your competitive advantage cannot be duplicated. Example: IN-N-OUT Burger vs. McDonald's.
- The above two items combined must be activities that can be **constantly improved**, nurtured, and altered to maintain that edge over your competition. Example: Wal-Mart vs. Kmart.

Now it is time to put your competitive advantage to the test.

Criteria for a Sustainable Competitive Advantage	Meets Criteria
How difficult will it be for competitors to match, offset, or leapfrog the expected advantages? Is it difficult to imitate?	
Do or will your customers see a consistent, superior difference between your product/service and those of my competitors?	
Does it build a company reputation and recognizable industry position?	
Can a unique resource be trumped by a different resource?	
Can the activities involved in creating the competitive advantage be constantly improved?	

STATE YOUR PURPOSE.

Be purpose-driven.

Mission Statement

PURPOSE: To define the company's purpose.

In light of all the needs we see, why do we exist as an organization? — Bob Beihl

A mission statement is a statement of the company's purpose. It spotlights what business a company is presently in and the customer needs it is presently endeavoring to meet. A mission statement deals with the present. It is a fixed vantage point, giving you perspective on where you are going. Your mission statement keeps your business headed in the right direction. It acts as the company's compass. With it, anyone in the organization can always judge the direction the company is moving in relation to its stated purpose. It explains why you do what you do within your company.

QUESTIONS TO ANSWER:
To write a mission statement, answer the questions:
  What is the purpose of your business?
  What do you intend to accomplish on behalf of your customers?
  In light of all the needs you see, why does your business exist?
  What needs does your organization exist to resolve?

CRITERIA:
An effective mission statement clearly defines who the customer is and what services and products the business intends to provide. It also serves as a guide for day-to-day operations and as the foundation for future decision-making. The following are criteria for an effective mission statement:

ACTION ITEMS
Write a working mission statement explaining the purpose of your company – the products/services you provide and the customers you serve.
MARKET FOCUS
A market-focused company starts with a mission statement that defines your company's purpose in terms of how you satisfy basic customer needs.

- **Focuses on Satisfying Customer Needs**
  A mission statement should focus the business on satisfying customer needs rather than on a product or service. It should describe results, not the methods of achieving those results.

Company	Product-Focused Definition	Market-Focused Definition
Southwest Airlines	We provide air travel.	We are dedicated to the highest quality of customer service delivered with a sense of warmth, friendliness, individual pride, and company spirit.

- **Tells "Who" Your Customers Are**
  Who is being satisfied? Your company should define the type of customers it wishes to serve. It should define which customer groups your business is targeting.

- **Explains "What" Customer Needs Your Company is Intending to Satisfy**
  Your company should define the particular needs of those customer groups it wishes to satisfy. A product or service becomes a business when it satisfies a need or a want.

- **Explains "How" Customer Needs are Satisfied**
  Your company should define the means or technology by which it will serve the customers and satisfy their needs.

- **Based on Your Core Competencies**
  Your company should base its mission on a competitively superior internal strength or resource that the company performs well in comparison to its competitors.
  - ❖ McDonald's core competence is providing low-cost food and fast service to large groups of customers.

- **Motivates and Inspires Employee Commitment**
  Your mission statement should be motivating. It should not be stated as making more sales or profits. Your employees need to feel that their work is significant and that it contributes to people's lives.

- **Realistic**
  Your mission statement should be realistic. You should avoid making the mission too narrow or too broad.

- **Specific, Short, Sharply Focused, and Memorable**
  Vague or generic mission statements lack resonance and meaning. It should be a precise statement of purpose. Describe the essence of the business in words your employees and customers can remember you by. It should "fit on a T-shirt".
  - ❖ "To serve the most vulnerable." (International Red Cross)

- **Clear and Easily Understood**
  Develop and write your mission statement on a "party level" (i.e. simple and clearly) so that you can quickly and briefly tell people you meet at a party or on airplanes why your company exists. At the same time it needs to give your company team a profoundly simple focus for everything it does as a business.

- **Says What the Company Wants to be Remembered For**
  In the end, a mission statement says what the company wants to be remembered for. How would the company want the world to think of them? This can provide a profoundly simple insight into your purpose for existing.

EXAMPLES:
The following are examples of company mission statements:
- ❖ **3M:** To solve unsolved problems innovatively.
- ❖ **Coca-Cola Company:** To benefit and refresh everyone it touches.
- ❖ **Mary Kay**: To give unlimited opportunity to women.
- ❖ **LCJ Marketing Source Inc.:** To make your company stand out in the crowd.
- ❖ **Small Business Technology Solutions:** To provide small businesses the functionality of big business, within a small business budget.
- ❖ **Professional Mortgage Services:** Our commitment to excellence and superior customer service is helping homeowners realize the American Dream every day.
- ❖ **Lord & Bryant Ltd.:** To assist individuals acquiring, exchanging, managing, and selling real property in the United States and overseas.
- ❖ **Merck***:* To preserve and improve human life.
- ❖ **Marriott**: To make people away from home feel they are among friends and really wanted.
- ❖ **Fannie Mae:** To strengthen the social fabric by democratizing home ownership.
- ❖ **Google:** To organize the world's information and make it universally accessible and useful.
- ❖ **Sony:** To experience the sheer joy of advancing and applying technology for the benefit of the public.
- ❖ **Sun Microsystems:** To solve complex network computing problems for governments, enterprises, and service providers.
- ❖ **University of Phoenix:** To educate working adults to develop the knowledge and skills that will enable them to achieve their professional goals, improve the productivity of their organizations, and provide leadership and service to their communities.

Worksheet: Developing Your Mission Statement

Directions: Write your mission statement and evaluate it.

MISSION STATEMENT

EVALUATION
Does your mission statement meet the criteria for an effective mission statement?

Criteria for an Effective Mission Statement	Yes	No
The mission statement is focused on satisfying *customer needs* rather than being focused on the product or service.		
The mission statement tells "who" your customers are, "what" customer needs your company wishes to satisfy and "how" customer needs are satisfied.		
The mission statement is based on your core competencies. *(A core competency is a competitively superior unique strength.)*		
The mission statement is motivating and inspires employee commitment.		
The mission statement is realistic.		
The mission statement is specific, short, sharply focused and memorable.		
The mission statement is clear and easily understood.		
The mission statement says what the company wants to be remembered for.		

BEFORE YOU MOVE ON:
Does your mission statement say what is the purpose of your business?

HELP PEOPLE SEE THE END STATE.

Visualize the future of your company in 10 years.

Describe it.
Touch it.
Feel it.
Live it.
Experience it.

Vision Statement & Organization-Wide Strategy

PURPOSE: To formulate a picture of what the company's future business makeup will be and where the company is headed.

Vision is the art of seeing things invisible.
— Jonathan Swift

Vision provides a clear mental picture of what your company will look like in 5 to 10 years from now. Forming a strategic vision should provide long-term direction, delineate what kind of enterprise the company is trying to become, and infuse the organization with a sense of purposeful action. It serves as a unifying focal point for everyone in the organization like a North Star. Your vision statement needs to be something you will achieve at some point in the future.

A vision provides the roadmap that delineates where the organization is going. It is the image of what your company's future makeup will be, the direction it is headed, the customer focus it should have, the market position it should try to occupy, the business activities to be pursued, and the capabilities it plans to develop. Vision is a guiding image of future success in the realization of the mission.

VISION STATEMENT

QUESTIONS TO ANSWER:
To write a vision statement, answer these questions:
> What will your business look like 5 to 10 years from now?
> What new things do you intend to pursue?
> What future customer needs do you want to satisfy?

CRITERIA:
The following is an explanation of the criteria for an effective vision statement:

- **Futurecasting: Provides a picture of what your business will look like in the future**
  A vision statement is a powerful picture of what the company's business will look like in 5 to 10 years.

- **Audacious: Represents a dream that is beyond what you think is possible**
  It represents the mountaintop your company is striving to reach. Visioning takes you out beyond your present reality.

- **Motivating: Clarifies the direction in which your organization needs to move**
  It clarifies the future direction the company and keeps everyone pushing forward to reach it.

- **Purpose-Driven: Worded to give employees a larger sense of purpose**
  It is worded to give employees a larger sense of purpose – so they see themselves as "building a cathedral" rather than "laying stones."

- **Inspiring: Worded in engaging language that inspires people**
  It creates a vivid image in people's heads that provokes emotion and excitement. It creates enthusiasm and poses a challenge that inspires and engages people in the company.

> **ACTION ITEMS**
> Write a vision statement that stands alone or is part of your mission statement. Think big! Then write the one or two guiding strategies you need to focus on to make this vision a reality.
>
> **MARKET FOCUS**
> Consider writing a vision statement that reflects your company in 3-5 years through the eyes of your customer.

- **Capitalizes on Core Competencies: Builds on your company's core competencies**
  It builds on what you have already established – company history, customer base, strengths, and unique capabilities, resources and assets.

EXAMPLES:
The following are examples of company vision statements:

- ❖ **McDonald's:** Our vision is to dominate the global foodservice industry.
- ❖ **Microsoft:** To enable people and businesses throughout the world to realize their full potential.
- ❖ **M3 Planning:** To start a strategy revolution.
- ❖ **Health Care for All:** All people in our state will have access to quality health care, regardless of ability to pay.
- ❖ **Pershing General Hospital:** To be the provider of first choice for our community and a leader in rural healthcare for Nevada.
- ❖ **Mortgage Company:** A mortgage loan company sets a goal of a 15-minute loan. (The industry average is several days.)
- ❖ **Heinz:** To be the world's premier food company, offering nutritious, superior tasting foods to people everywhere.
- ❖ **Novo Nordisk:** To be the world's leading diabetes care company.
- ❖ **Visa:** Our vision for the future of payments is a world in which buyers and sellers can conduct commerce anywhere, anytime, and in any way they choose.
- ❖ **DuPont:** To be the world's most dynamic science company, creating sustainable solutions essential to a better, safer and healthier life for people everywhere.
- ❖ **Chemtura:** To be the world's best specialty chemicals company.
- ❖ **BearingPoint:** To be the world's most influential and respected business advisor and systems integrator.

ORGANIZATION-WIDE STRATEGY
While strategies are embedded in all elements of your strategic plan, consider listing the top one to two strategies or long-term activities your company needs to pursue in order to achieve its vision. Your strategies are the general methods you intend to use to reach your vision. A strategy is a general statement(s) that guides and explains how you will get to your vision. It can be a guiding statement for the ongoing life of the company or for the year.

QUESTIONS TO ANSWER:
A strategy answers the question "how." To write strategies, answer these questions:
  How will we achieve our vision?
  What key initiatives do we need to pursue over the long term?

EXAMPLES:
The following are examples of a guiding strategy:

- ❖ **Starbucks:** To build the brand one cup at a time, based on three key ingredients: the quality of the coffee, our own retail stores, and selective brand extensions.
- ❖ **Computer Consulting Company:** To lay the foundation for growth this year.
- ❖ **The Economics Development Authority of Western Nevada:** to move towards economic development plus to increase the base of companies contributing to the region's measurable quality of life to ensure long-term vitality of the community.

Worksheet: Developing Your Vision Statement

Directions: Write your vision statement. Then use the criteria described on the previous page to evaluate the effectiveness of your vision statement. Place a dot on the appropriate axis to rate your vision statement against each corresponding criteria. Then connect all your dots within the circle. Next, shade in the connected dot area. The shaded area represents the overall effectiveness of the vision. The closer it is to the perimeter, the more effective your vision statement is; the closer it is to the center of the circle, the less effective it is. Then write one or two guiding strategies.

VISION STATEMENT & GUIDING STRATEGY

EVALUATION
This visual tool can be used to assess the effectiveness of your vision statement. It is a simple tool to help you see the important aspects of vision. It also helps you look at your vision statement from different perspectives.

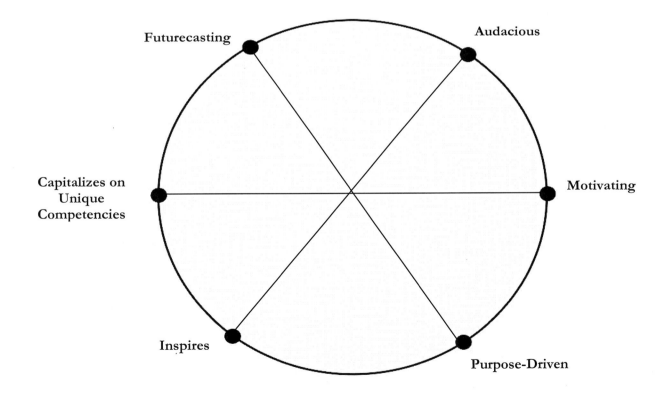

BEFORE YOU MOVE ON:
Is your vision statement a picture of your company's future?

YOUR ORGANIZATION IS A COLLECTION OF BELIEFS.

A solid foundation
is key to building an organization
that will grow, succeed, excel, and prosper.

Beliefs are the core values and principles we live by.
When they are shared with others, a bond
is created. A culture is formed, becoming
a solid foundation.

Core Values

PURPOSE: To identify the authentic core values and beliefs that the company is truly committed to.

The values of any organization control priorities, provide the foundation for formulating goals, and set the tone and direction of the organization. – Lyle Schaller

Values are enduring, passionate, and distinctive core beliefs. They are guiding principles that never change. Values are why we do what we do and what we stand for. Values are deeply held convictions, priorities, and underlying assumptions which influence our attitudes and behaviors. They have intrinsic value and importance to those inside the organization. Your core values are part of your strategic foundation.

More and more companies are articulating the core beliefs and values underlying their business activities. Strong values account for why some companies gain a reputation for such strategic traits as leadership, product innovation, dedication to superior craftsmanship, a good company to work for, and total customer satisfaction. A company's values can dominate the kind of strategic moves it considers or rejects. When values and beliefs are deeply ingrained and widely shared by managers and employees, they become a way of life within the company, and they mold company strategy.

QUESTIONS TO ANSWER:
To identify your company's values, answer these questions:
    What are the core values and beliefs of your company?
    What values and beliefs guide your daily interactions?
    What are you and your people really committed to?
    What are the non-negotiables?

> **ACTION ITEMS**
> Write your company's core values.
>
> **MARKET FOCUS**
> A market-focused company links their core values to satisfying their customer's needs.

EXAMPLES:
The following are examples of company core values and the strategy based on these core values:
- ❖ Hewlett-Packard
  Core Values: Trust and respect for employees, provide customers with products and services of the greatest value, individual initiative and creativity, teamwork, community contribution and responsibility, and profitable growth.
  Strategy based on Core Values: Attract top university graduates and provide a creative environment in which to work, have employees feel that senior management works *for* them, provide customers with effective solutions to their problems through their innovative products and new technology, avoid the use of long-term debt to finance growth, large R&D investment that fuels innovative offerings.

- ❖ Sony
  Core Values: Elevate the Japanese culture and national status, be a pioneer, encourage individual ability and creativity.
  Strategy based on Core Values: Create leading electronic products in the U.S. and worldwide, have a recognizable brand name, produce innovative quality Japanese products.

- ❖ Starbucks Coffee Company
  Core Values: Passion for what we do, integrity in how we do it, pride in winning, respect for our partners, entrepreneurial spirit.
  Strategy based on Core Values: To provide an uplifting experience that enriches people's lives. Build the brand one cup at a time based on the quality of the coffee, own retail stores, and brand extension.

Worksheet: Identifying Your Company Values

The purpose of this exercise is to help you identify the authentic core values and beliefs that your company is truly committed to.

Direction: Write down 3 to 5 authentic core values and beliefs that your company is truly committed to. Describe each core value. Evaluate each core value listed against the questions under "Identifying Authentic Core Values" below.

CORE VALUES

EVALUATION

Identifying Authentic Core Values	Yes	No
If you were to start a new company, would this core value be part of its foundation?		
Will you continue to stand by and hold this value no matter what happens in the competitive environment?		
Are you willing to stand by this value no matter what the cost – for example lost clients or lost revenue?		
Do you believe that employees who do not share this value should continue to be part of your company?		
Do you demonstrate this core value in your leadership?		
Would you sell your company before giving up this core value?		
Do you apply this core value in your personal activities?		
If you could do anything in the world, would you continue to apply this core value to your productive activities?		

BEFORE YOU MOVE ON:
Are you committed to these core values?

PRODUCE HOLISTIC VISION DELIVERABLES.

That's exactly what objectives are.
Statements about how you will deliver your vision.
In a complete, holistic, integrated, clear, achievable method.

Strategic Objectives

PURPOSE: To get you from where you are (your mission and values) to where you are going (your vision).

Which comes first – objectives or goals? How do they work together? This is probably the most widely debated part of strategic planning. So what is the difference between them and how do you use them? Every person you ask will provide a different answer. My suggestion is to ignore the semantics and focus on establishing a framework. What matters is having a combination of long-term and short-term markers to keep your organization moving in the right direction. Think of the following hierarchy:

Mission: States "where you are now." This is the underlying "why" you are in business in the first place.
Vision: States "where you are going." Everything your company does is focused on achieving your vision.
Strategic Objectives: Explains "How you will get there." They are long-term, broad and continuous activities that state how you will achieve your vision.
Goals: These are one-year markers that support your long-term strategic objectives.
Action Items: These explain how your short-term goals are accomplished by whom and by when.

Objectives are the general areas in which your effort is directed to drive your organization from its mission to its vision. Think of objectives as broad umbrella categories. Objectives state the broad direction; goals then operationalize that direction. They are the continuous strategic activities necessary to achieve your vision. They define what your business is intending to accomplish both programmatically and organizationally. Objectives work towards converting your mission into actions that will accomplish your vision and help sustain your competitive advantage.

QUESTIONS TO ANSWER:
To write an objective, answer the questions:
> What areas do you need to be involved in to accomplish your mission?
> In what areas will you continue being actively involved in during the next five plus years?

CRITERIA:
Use the following criteria when evaluating each objective:
- Is my objective broad?
- Is my objective continuous, ongoing, and non-dated?
- Does it convert my mission/vision into action?
- Does it help to sustain my competitive advantage?

TYPES OF OBJECTIVES:
The Balanced Scorecard (see Step 12) is an excellent management tool that ensures you have a holistic and balanced strategy as well as a way to track performance. To have a balanced and holistic strategy, organizations must have objectives and goals in the following four key areas:

ACTION ITEMS
Write at least one objective in each of the following areas:
- Financial – Your bottom line
- Customer – How you will satisfy them
- Internal/Operational – Best practices you need in place
- People/Learning – Staying ahead of the curve

MARKET FOCUS
Your Customer objectives are core. They drive Financial objectives and are supported by Internal/Operational and People/Learning objectives.

Financial Objectives – How will we look to our stakeholders?
Financial objectives focus on achieving acceptable profitability in a company's pursuit of its mission, vision, long-term health, and ultimate survival. Best strategy practices suggest there be at least two objectives in this area. For example:
- ❖ *Revenue Growth*: To exceed $20 million in the next ten years.
- ❖ *Productivity Improvement*: To drive net profit to more than 10% in the next 7 to 10 years.

Customer Objectives – How do we provide value to our customers?
Customer objectives support the financial objectives. They focus on the company's intent to sustain and improve the company's competitive strength and long-term market position through creating customer value. These objectives focus on meeting the needs of the customer through products and services. There should be at least two or three objectives focusing on providing over-arching customer value. For example:

❖ *Customer Retention:* Maintain existing customer base by increasing repeat customers.
❖ *Customer Acquisition*: Increase our market share by gaining new customers in a foreign market.
❖ *Customer Service*: Improve our service approach for new and existing customers.

Internal/Operational Objectives – To satisfy our customers, what processes must we excel at?
Internal/Operational objectives support the customer and financial objectives. They focus on processes that have an impact on creating customer value and satisfaction. These objectives focus on maintaining the firm's core competencies. They represent internal management activities, processes and operational functions needed to support the products and services. There will generally be four or more objectives in this area. For example:

❖ *Product Management*: To have all product meet standard of excellence guidelines.
[Note: Some businesses prefer to list each product as a separate objective.]
❖ *Operations Management*: To continually improve process to realize efficiencies. (An organization probably will have 2 or more operations management objectives.)
❖ *Technology Management*: To successfully implement and realize benefits from our computer and software systems.
❖ *Customer Management*: To execute and maintain a CRM process that is producing results.
❖ *Marketing Management*: To continuously broaden our customer database by obtaining new information on customer characteristics and needs.
❖ *Channel Management*: To aggressively strengthen our upstream channels.

People/Learning Objectives – To excel at our processes, how must we learn and improve?
People/Learning objectives drive everything else in your plan. Without your team, you don't have an organization. These objectives focus on the development of people, increasing the company's knowledge base, continuous improvement through innovation, and learning best practices, so that they are continually on the cutting edge. The internal processes and customer value-creating activities cannot happen without the right people, the right skill sets and appropriate environment. Best strategy practices would suggest a minimum of three objectives. For example:

❖ *Training*: To continually train staff for necessary skills to be successful as well as develop leadership abilities.
❖ *Culture*: To align incentives and staff rewards with performance.
❖ *People:* To hire, develop and maintain the right people, in the right "seats on the bus."
❖ *Knowledge:* To continually learn and adopt current best practices.

CAUSE AND EFFECT RELATIONSHIP BETWEEN STRATEGIC OBJECTIVES

The logic goes like this: If you want to generate additional revenue, you need to provide value to your customers. In order to provide value to your customers, you must have internal business processes to create that value. And in order for your business processes to function, you need people who are skilled and knowledgeable. That is the essence of having a balanced strategic organization. In the example below, you can clearly see the cause and effect relationship between your organization's actions.

Example

In this example, you can clearly see the cause and effect relationship between a company's actions: Tammy Tantalizing Tacos' top line financial goal is to increase her annual revenue by 10%. How will she achieve her financial goal? To sell more tacos. In order to sell more tacos, what must she do from her customers' perspective? Provide great customer service. And what does she need to do to deliver great customer service? Have efficient processes that deliver food quickly. And how does she excel at quick food delivery? By having well-trained employees.

Worksheet: Writing Strategic Objectives

As previously mentioned, objectives are long-term, broad, non-measurable, and continuous. Objectives are the general areas that drive your organization from its mission to its vision while sustaining your competitive advantage.

BRAINSTORMING

Directions: Using a piece of paper draw a circle that represents your competitive advantage. Surround it with a second circle that represents your mission and vision. Then think of all the actions, strategies, resources, alliances, and processes by which you can bring action to your mission and vision statements. Look for broad areas in the brainstorming map you just created. Be sure to think about the four main areas of your company: Financial, Customer, Internal/Operational and People/Learning.

LONG-TERM OBJECTIVES

Directions: Based on your company's competitive advantage, mission and vision, look for broad areas that will move your company from *motive* to *action*. Write down 2 or more broad objectives for each of the four areas: Financial, Customer, Internal/Operational and People/Learning. For examples, refer to "Types of Objectives" on the previous pages.

Financial

Customer

Internal/Operational

People/Learning

BEFORE YOU MOVE ON:

Is each objective broad, non-measurable, and continuous?
Does each objective work towards converting your mission into actions that will accomplish your vision and help sustain your competitive advantage?

FUTURECAST.

Companies spend time predicting what sales will be like in the future. But we spend little time actually thinking in any serious way about that future – it is the underlying dynamics, the sweeping trajectory of new competition, the way customers will evolve, the collision course one industry may be on with another.

Take this time to "futurecast" – to examine the world your company will do business in 2030 to get a different view of your challenge. Dream. Build. Expand. When you journey back to this planning session, you'll have a new perspective on how to handle the challenges at hand.

Internal and External Assessment

PURPOSE: To assess the particular strengths, weaknesses, opportunities, and threats that are strategically important to your company.

Results are gained by exploiting opportunities, not by solving problems. — Peter Drucker

An internal and external assessment is also known as a SWOT. The SWOT (Strengths, Weaknesses, Opportunities, Threats) analysis helps you look critically at your company. The SWOT is a balance sheet of your strategic position right now and is powerful for strategy development. However, like any planning tool, the SWOT is only as good as the information it contains. A good understanding of your strengths and weaknesses, your market opportunities, and the external threats are essential to the assessment. Gathering information from your customers about the effectiveness of your products/services and company are essential for the SWOT to identify key issues. The purpose of a SWOT is to help produce a good fit between your company's internal resources and capabilities and your external environment.

QUESTIONS TO ANSWER:
Assess your company by answering these questions:
   What are your company capabilities (functions)?
   What are your company resources – skills, people,
      capabilities, functions, assets?
Assess your market by answering these questions:
   What is happening externally that will affect your company?
   Who are your customers?
   What are the strengths and weaknesses of each competitor?
   What are the driving forces behind sales trends?
   What are important and potentially important markets?
   What world events might affect your company?

ACTION ITEMS
Assess the internal and external factors that affect your company.
▪ Build on your strengths
▪ Shore up your weaknesses
▪ Capitalize on your opportunities
▪ Recognize your threats
MARKET FOCUS
The information you gather in this step about your market, competitors, customers, and environment will be used to set your goals. The more you learn about your market and use it to drive your company, the more successful you will be.

CRITERIA:
In the analysis, you bring together all of your internal factors, strengths and weaknesses, as well as your external factors, opportunities and threats. Strengths and weaknesses are factors that you can control and affect. Opportunities and threats are outside of your control, that you can either try to take advantage of or minimize.

Internal Assessment
The Internal Assessment examines strengths and weaknesses that exist within the company. These internal factors give an organization certain advantages and disadvantages in meeting the needs of its target customers. A company is market focused when it uses its strengths to meet customer requirements.

   ▪ **Strengths** refer to what your company does well. It gives your business an advantage in meeting the needs of its target markets. An analysis of company strengths should be market and customer focused, because strengths are only meaningful when they assist the business in meeting customer needs. Strengths give the company enhanced competitiveness.

   ▪ **Weaknesses** refer to any limitations a company faces in developing or implementing a strategy. A weakness is something a company lacks or does poorly in comparison to others, or a condition that puts it at a disadvantage. Weaknesses should also be examined from a customer perspective, because customers often perceive weaknesses that a company cannot see.

External Assessment

The External Assessment examines opportunities and threats that exist in the marketplace. Both opportunities and threats exist independently of the company. A company should recognize them by trying to take advantage of the opportunities and by trying to minimize the threats.

- **Opportunities** are situations that exist but must be acted on if the business is to benefit from them. Opportunities most relevant to a company are those that offer important avenues for profitable growth, those where a company has the most potential for competitive development, and those that match up well with the financial and organizational resource capabilities that the company already possesses or can acquire.

- **Threats** refer to external conditions or barriers that may prevent a company from reaching its objectives.

SWOT ANALYSIS PARTS

There are four parts to complete a SWOT analysis:

External Assessment: Analyzes your company's *opportunities* and *threats*.
Part One: Environmental Analysis looks at environmental trends affecting your company.
Part Two: Market Analysis assesses market trends.
Part Three: Competitive Analysis sizes up your competitor's strengths and weaknesses.

Internal Assessment: Analyzes your company's *strengths* and *weaknesses*.
Part Four: Internal Assessment analyzes your company's strengths and weaknesses.

SWOT ANALYSIS OVERVIEW

The Internal and External Assessments will be summarized in a SWOT matrix to help you visualize the analysis. When executing this analysis, it is important to understand how these elements work together. When a company matches internal strengths to external opportunities, it creates core competencies in meeting the needs of its customers. In addition, the company should act to convert its internal weaknesses into strengths and manage external threats appropriately. When planning, remember to build on your strengths; shore up your weaknesses; capitalize on your opportunities; and recognize your threats.

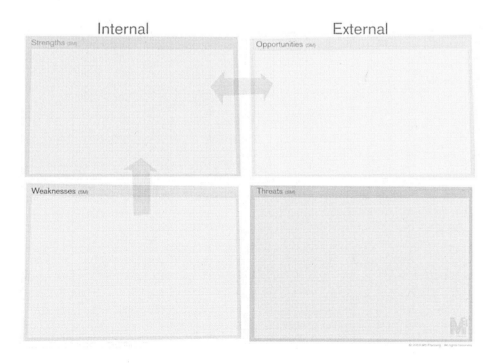

Worksheet: Assessing Your Internal and External Environment

The SWOT consists of an External Assessment where you will look at environmental trends, market trends and competitive trends. It also consists of an Internal Assessment where you will assess your competitive resources and capabilities.

Directions:

Step 1 External Assessment: Analyze your company's **opportunities and threats**.
> List the external opportunities and threats that may impact your company. Use the questions under Part One: Environmental Analysis, Part Two: Market Analysis, and Part Three: Competitive Analysis as a tool to help you better understand your marketplace. Based on your answers to these questions, classify them under *Opportunities* or *Threats*. Then summarize your answers on the "Internal and External Assessment Summary" found at the end of this step.

Step 2 Internal Assessment: Analyze your company's **strengths** and **weaknesses**.
> List the internal strengths and weaknesses that may impact your company. Use the *Value Creating Activities* statements as a tool to help you better analyze your company. First rate how well your company performs each value creating activity. Then rate how important each activity is in the primary market you operate in. Based on your answers to these statements, use the "Internal Assessment Chart" to graph each of your answers. Then summarize Key *Strengths* and Key *Weaknesses* on the "Internal and External Assessment Summary" found at the end of this step. Your analysis will be more accurate if you vary your ratings. Evaluate your company critically.

Step 3 Internal and External Assessment Summary: Add to the list.
> List additional strengths you want to focus on, weaknesses you want to shore up, opportunities you want to capitalize on, and threats you need to acknowledge to items developed in Steps 1 and 2.

EXTERNAL ASSESSMENT

Part One: Environmental Analysis
Purpose: Identify environmental trends and events that have the potential to affect your company.
- What are the economic and demographic changes that could affect your company in your market?
- What are the technological developments or trends that could affect your industry?
- What political and legal changes might impact your industry?
- What are the current/emerging trends or components of society that will impact your company?
- What are the key areas of uncertainty that have the potential to impact your company?

Part Two: Market Analysis
Purpose: Identify the primary market your business competes in, the market trends, and opportunities.
- What is the primary market you compete in? (Geographic, functionally or industry)
- What is profitable in your market? What is not profitable in your market?
- Is the customer base growing or shrinking?
- Why are customers using your product/service? What is the value provided?
- Are there substitute products/services? What are they?
- Is the power of your suppliers growing or shrinking?
- Are there opportunities in your primary market that you could capitalize on?
- Are there current or growing threats that you need to be aware of?
- What are two markets your company does not currently operate in that are potential opportunities?

Part Three: Competitive Analysis
Purpose: Identify companies you compete against and their characteristics.
- List your existing and/or potential competitors by name or group. What are each one's strengths and weaknesses? Are these opportunities or threats to your company?
- What are your competitors' competitive advantages?
- What is happening with competitors? Is competition growing or shrinking?
- Are there new competitors emerging?

INTERNAL ASSESSMENT
Part Four: Internal Assessment

	Relative Strength	Strategic Importance
Directions: Rate each activity on a scale of 1 to 10 (1 = low, 10 = high). Only rate measures that are relevant to your company.		
Value Creating Activities	How good is your company at...?	How critical is this activity in your market?
Financial Activities (blue diamond)		
Maximizing sales		
Improving profit margins		
Maximizing cash flow		
Maximizing net profit		
Increasing overall performance of the company		
Strategic Customer Activities (pink square)		
Improving awareness of the company's products/services		
Building customer relationships		
Reducing customer complaints		
Improving customer satisfaction		
Strategic Marketplace Activities (yellow triangle)		
Increasing market share of principal product/service		
Increasing repeat business		
Attracting new customers		
Improving customer profitability		
Retaining current customers		
Internal Business Activities (aqua square)		
Improving operational efficiencies		
Improving quality of products/services		
Reducing order-to-delivery cycle time		
Minimizing defects in products/services		
Reducing response time for customer complaints		
Effective use of promotional budgets		
Staff Learning Activities (red square)		
Hiring qualified employees		
Developing and training employees		
Enhancing employee productivity		
Building employee satisfaction		
Retaining current employees		
Innovation Activities (brown circle)		
Developing more business from existing markets		
Adding more value to existing products/services		
Bringing new products/services to market		
Increasing level of innovation in products/services		
Entering new market segments		

INTERNAL ASSESSMENT CHART

Directions
1. Based on your answers to the previous questions, chart the *Relative Strength* and *Strategic Importance* of each value-creating activity on the chart below.
2. List the *Key Strengths and Key Weaknesses* on the "Internal and External Assessment Summary" on the next page.

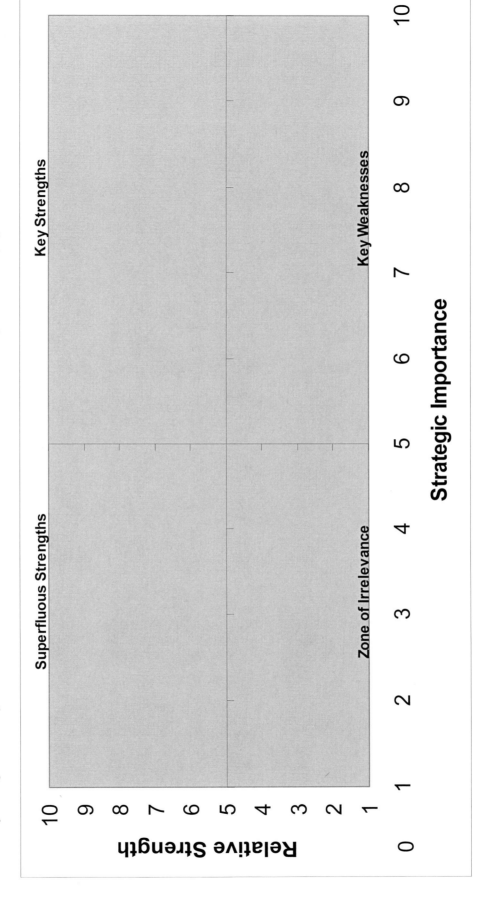

Key: Financial – blue diamond   Internal Business – aqua square
       Strategic Customer – pink square   Staff Learning – red square
       Strategic Marketplace – yellow triangle   Innovation – brown circle

41

Internal and External Assessment Summary

External

Opportunities (SM)

Threats (SM)

Internal

Strengths (SM)

Weaknesses (SM)

VISUALIZE SHAKING YOUR CUSTOMER'S HAND.

Know your customers likes, dislikes, needs, wants, birthdays, anniversaries, style, titles, beliefs, behaviors, perspectives, politics, dreams, loyalty, lifestyle, personality, social status, motivations, aspirations, expectations, irritations, opportunities…and the list goes on…

You can't see what you don't know.
Visualize your customers so you can see them with 100 percent clarity.
They are the reason you are in business.

Know your customers.

Customer Groups

PURPOSE: To identify groups of your customers that have similar characteristics and choosing groups to focus on.

What I knew yesterday is not enough for today. I'm not responding fast enough for my customer.
— Feargal Quinn, Superquinn

The purpose of this section is to identify Customer groups. If you want to move your company from being average to successful, you need to meet your customers' needs and wants better than your competitors do. Customer-focused companies recognize that they cannot appeal to all buyers in the marketplace or at least not to all buyers in the same way. Buyers are too numerous, too widely scattered, and too varied in their needs and buying practices.

Rather than trying to compete in the entire market, each company must identify parts of the market that it can serve best and most profitably. The most effective way to do this is to group customers that respond in a similar way to a product or service offering. Understanding and targeting Customer groups is critical to developing a sustainable competitive advantage. Thus, we will identify, develop a descriptive customer profile and a positioning statement for each target Customer group.

QUESTIONS TO ANSWER:
Answer the following questions to help identify your target Customer groups:
    What Customer groups are you targeting?
    Who are your biggest customers?
    Do your customers fall into any logical groups based on
        needs, motivations, or characteristics?
    Are there one or two characteristics that will help you
        group your customers? (geographic, price, need, etc.)
    Have you described them well enough to picture
        shaking their hand?

> **ACTION ITEMS**
> Divide your customers and potential customers into groups based on similar characteristics. Remember: Customers in a group must be measurable, reachable, substantial, and differentiable.
>
> **MARKET FOCUS**
> In order to achieve your Financial and Customer objectives, focus on your customers. Who are they?

CRITERIA:
After you have identified your Customer groups, evaluate them based on the following criteria:
- Can you *measure* the size of the group?
- Can you *reach* this group through clear communication channels?
- Are there *enough customers* in the group to make it profitable?
- Will this group *respond differently* to product and service offerings than other groups identified?

TARGETING YOUR CUSTOMER GROUPS:
The following are three steps for targeting Customer groups:
1. *Grouping*:
   - Group Name - name your distinct Customer groups.
   - Needs - divide the market into distinct groups of buyers on the basis of their needs and wants.
   - Characteristics - divide the market into distinct groups of buyers on the basis of characteristics.
   - Profile - develop a customer profile for each group based on their needs and characteristics.
2. *Targeting*: Evaluate each Customer group's attractiveness and select one or more groups.
3. *Positioning*: Create a value proposition and image so that you occupy a unique and distinctive place in the "mind of the target market". A positioning statement guides all your marketing efforts directed at the target Customer group. It is the core message you want to deliver in every medium and everything you do.

EXAMPLES:

Customer Profile
Creating a good customer profile that requires you visualize your customers with 100 percent clarity. The following are examples of good and bad customer profiles:

Bad Example:	*Good Example:*	*Better Example:*
Small businesses located Oregon	Small businesses located Oregon that are in the auto industry	Small body shops seeking rapid insurance reimbursement in Oregon
All agencies in the marketing industry	All agencies in the marketing industry billing less than $10 million annually	An agency focusing on public relations for local and state government community programs
Field sales people constantly on the road	Field sales people earning between $50-$100K who are looking to purchase a new car in the next year	Field sales people earning between $50-$100K who are image conscious first movers and are looking to purchase a sports car in the next year

Best Example: Anthropologie – A nationwide retail store:
"A female about 30 to 45 years old, college or post-graduate education, married with kids, professional or ex-professional, annual household income of $150,000 to $200,000. She's well-read and well-traveled. She is very aware -- she gets our references, whether it's to a town in Europe or to a book or a movie. She's urban minded. She's into cooking, gardening, and wine. She has a natural curiosity about the world. She's relatively fit. Her identity is a tangle of connections to activities, places, interests, values, and aspirations.

The Anthropologie customer is affluent but not materialistic. She's focused on building a nest but hankers for exotic travel. She'd like to be a domestic. She's in tune with trends, but she's a confident individualist when it comes to style. She lives in the suburbs but would never consider herself a suburbanite." *– Fast Company*

Positioning Statement
Here are a handful of positioning statements from large and small companies. Sometimes a positioning statement sounds like a tag line or a slogan. That's fine, but remember that the purpose of a positioning statement is not to be cute. Rather its purpose is to help guide all of your activities associated with a specific Customer group. You can turn it into a marketing message in the future.

- ❖ **Mercedes Benz:** Engineered like no other car in the world.
- ❖ **Wharton Business School:** The only business school that trains managers who are global, cross-functional, good leaders, and leveraged by technology.
- ❖ **BMW:** The ultimate driving machine.
- ❖ **Southwest Airlines:** The short-haul, no-frills, and low-priced airline.
- ❖ **Midwest Express:** All the creature comforts and calm, refined air service at competitive prices.
- ❖ **Avis:** We are only Number 2, so we try harder!
- ❖ **Famous Footwear:** The value shoe store for families.
- ❖ **The Heidel House Resort:** The place to reconnect with loved ones.
- ❖ **Northern Nevada Business Weekly:** The only source for local business news.

Worksheet: Targeting Your Customer Groups

The purpose of this worksheet is to develop a Customer Profile of your customers and potential customers. Remember your customers may be consumers, businesses or both.

Directions: Based on the instructions below, complete a "Customer Group" worksheet for *each* distinct group of customers. You may have one or several Customer groups. Create a Customer Profile for *each* group you will target.

Step 1: GROUPING

Group Name
Name your target Customer group.

Customer Needs
List the needs or wants of this Customer group. Customer groups can be segmented based on similar needs, motivation, or behavior. You may also choose to approach this by picking one product/ service that your company provides in meeting the needs of this group. For example, the U.S. car market can be segmented by product type (luxury car, sedan, minivans, sports cars) and customer needs (convenience, style, cost, reliability).

Customer Characteristics
List the characteristics that describe this group. To help you group your target customers, a detailed list of major categories of characteristics is provided at the end of this section. If you have a consumer product or service the major categories of characteristics are: demographic, geographic, lifestyle, and usage. If you have a business-to-business product or service, the major categories are: demographic, environmental, operating variables, purchasing approaches, situational factors, and personal characteristics. Remember there is no best way to segment a market; it requires your creativity.

Customer Profile
Create a customer profile that uniquely describes this Customer group. Each customer profile should be descriptive enough that it enables you to "shake the imaginary hand" of this group. Add any descriptive words that you did not include under customer needs and customer characteristics.

Step 2: TARGETING
Evaluate your Customer group's attractiveness:
- How big is this Customer group and what is the growth potential?
- Is this group substantial? Can you reach these customers?
- Does targeting this group leverage your competitive advantage? Do you have the resources?

Evaluate the financial feasibility:
- Is this group profitable? Projected Revenue – Estimated Expenses = Profit
  If so, then determine the projected Revenue.

Select groups your company can compete in successfully. Combine any groups where the key success factors are similar. For each group formulate a single value creating strategy.

Step 3: POSITIONING STATEMENT
Create a company value proposition and image so that you occupy a unique and distinctive place in the "mind" of the target Customer group. When your customer thinks of your company, what do you want to come to mind? This positioning statement is the core message you want to deliver through your messaging and communication.

Customer Group

Step 1: GROUPING

Group Name: _____

Customer Needs:
For this Customer group, list their needs and wants.

Customer Profile:
Create a Customer Profile that uniquely describes this group. Use the *Customer Needs* and *Customer Characteristics* to create the profile. Be descriptive enough that it enables you to shake the imaginary hand of this Customer group.

Customer Characteristics:
List the characteristics that describe this group.

Step 2: TARGETING
Evaluate your Customer group's attractiveness:
- How big is this target Customer group and what is the growth potential?
  Estimated number of customers:_____   Estimated Annual Growth:_____
- Is this group substantial? Can you reach these customers?
- Does targeting this group leverage your competitive advantage? Do you have the resources?

Evaluate the financial feasibility:
- Is this group profitable? Projected Revenue – Estimated Expenses = Profit
  If so, then what is the Estimated Revenue this year from this group? _____
  (number of customers x aver. sale per customer x number of sales per customer per year = Revenue)

Step 3: POSITIONING STATEMENT
Create a company value proposition and image so that you occupy a unique and distinctive place in the "mind" of the target Customer group. When your customer thinks of your company, what do you want to come to mind?

Positioning Statement:

Customer Group

Step 1: GROUPING

Group Name: _____

Customer Needs:
For this Customer group, list their
needs and wants.

Customer Profile:
Create a Customer Profile that uniquely
describes this group. Use the *Customer
Needs* and *Customer Characteristics* to
create the profile. Be descriptive enough that
it enables you to shake the imaginary hand of
this Customer group.

Customer Characteristics:
List the characteristics that describe
this group.

Step 2: TARGETING
Evaluate your Customer group's attractiveness:
- How big is this target Customer group and what is the growth potential?
  Estimated number of customers:_____   Estimated Annual Growth:_____
- Is this group substantial? Can you reach these customers?
- Does targeting this group leverage your competitive advantage? Do you have the resources?

Evaluate the financial feasibility:
- Is this group profitable? Projected Revenue – Estimated Expenses = Profit
  If so, then what is the Estimated Revenue this year from this group? _____
  (number of customers x aver. sale per customer x number of sales per customer per year = Revenue)

Step 3: POSITIONING STATEMENT
Create a company value proposition and image so that you occupy a unique and distinctive place in the
"mind" of the target Customer group. When your customer thinks of your company, what do you want to
come to mind?

Positioning Statement:

Customer Group

Step 1: GROUPING

Group Name: _____

Customer Needs:
For this Customer group, list their
needs and wants.

Customer Profile:
Create a Customer Profile that uniquely
describes this group. Use the *Customer
Needs* and *Customer Characteristics* to
create the profile. Be descriptive enough that
it enables you to shake the imaginary hand of
this Customer group.

Customer Characteristics:
List the characteristics that describe
this group.

Step 2: TARGETING
Evaluate your Customer group's attractiveness:
- How big is this target Customer group and what is the growth potential?
  Estimated number of customers:_____   Estimated Annual Growth:_____
- Is this group substantial? Can you reach these customers?
- Does targeting this group leverage your competitive advantage? Do you have the resources?

Evaluate the financial feasibility:
- Is this group profitable? Projected Revenue – Estimated Expenses = Profit
  If so, then what is the Estimated Revenue this year from this group? _____
  (number of customers x aver. sale per customer x number of sales per customer per year = Revenue)

Step 3: POSITIONING STATEMENT
Create a company value proposition and image so that you occupy a unique and distinctive place in the
"mind" of the target Customer group. When your customer thinks of your company, what do you want to
come to mind?

Positioning Statement:

Customer Characteristic Variables for Consumer Markets

DEMOGRAPHIC	
Age	Under 6, 6-11, 12-19, 20-34, 35-49, 50-64, 65+
Generation	Generation Y's, Generation Xers, baby boomers
Gender	Male, female
Income	Under $10,000; $10,000-$15,000; $15,000-$20,000; $20,000-$30,000; $30,000-$50,000; $50,000-$75,000; $75,000-$100,000; over $100,000
Family size	1-2, 3, 4, 5, 5+
Life cycle	Young, single; young, married, no kids; young, married, youngest kid under 6; young, married, youngest kid over 6; older, married, no kids; older married, kids at home; older, married, no kids at home; older single
Occupation	Professional & technical, managers, officials, proprietors, clerical, sales, craftspeople, supervisors, farmers, retired, students, homemakers, unemployed
Education	Grade school or less, some high school, high school graduate, some college, college graduate, graduate work
Religion	Catholic, Protestant, Evangelical, Jewish, Muslim, Hindu
Race	White, Black, Asian, Hispanic
Ethnicity	North American, South American, Latin American, British, French, German, Italian, Japanese, etc.
Social class	Lower lowers, upper lowers, working class, middle class, upper middles, lower uppers, upper uppers
GEOGRAPHIC	
Country region	Pacific, Mountain, West North Central, West South Central, East north Central, East South Central, South Atlantic, Middle Atlantic, New England
City size	Under 10,000; 10,000-50,000; 50,000-200,000; 200,000-500,000
Climate	Humid, dry, hot, rainy, cold
Density	Urban, suburban, rural
LIFESTYLE	
Lifestyle	Innovators, Thinkers, Achievers, Experiencers, Believers, Strivers, Makers, Survivors (VALS™ Segments)
Personality	Compulsive, gregarious, authoritarian, ambitious
Political views	Republican, Democratic, Independent, Libertarian
USAGE	
Occasions	Regular, special (critical life events or transitions)
Benefits sought	Quality, service, economy, speed
User status	Nonuser, ex-user, potential user, first-time user, regular user
Usage rate	Light user, medium user, heavy user
Loyalty status	None, medium, strong, absolute (hard-core, split, shifting, switcher)

Adapted from: Kotler, Philip and Gary Armstrong, *Principles of Marketing*, Tenth Edition. Upper Saddle River, NJ: Pearson/Prentice Hall, 2004.

Customer Characteristic Variables for Business Markets

DEMOGRAPHIC	
Industry	Which industries that buy this product should we focus on?
Company size	What size companies should we focus on?
Location	What geographical areas should we focus on?
ENVIRONMENTAL	
Economic developments	What economic development should we focus on?
Supply conditions	What type of supply conditions should we focus on?
Technological change	What technological change should we focus on?
Political and regulatory developments	Do we need to focus on any political and regulatory developments?
Competitive developments	What competitive developments should we focus on?
Culture and customs	Should we focus on a specific culture and/or custom?
OPERATING VARIABLES	
Technology	What customer technologies should we focus on?
User-nonuser status	Should we focus on heavy, medium, or light users or nonusers?
Customer capabilities	Should we focus on customers needing many services or few services?
PURCHASING APPROACHES	
Purchasing-function organization	Should we focus on companies with highly centralized or decentralized purchasing?
Power structure	Should we focus on companies that are engineering, financially or marketing dominated?
Nature of existing relationships	Should we focus on companies with which we already have strong relationships or simply go after the most desirable companies?
General purchase policies	Should we focus on companies that prefer leasing? Service contracts? Systems purchases? Sealed bidding?
Purchasing criteria	Should we focus on companies that are seeking quality? Service? Price?
SITUATIONAL FACTORS	
Urgency	Should we focus on companies that need quick delivery or service?
Specific application	Should we focus on certain applications of our product rather than all applications?
Size of order	Should we focus on large or small orders?
PERSONAL CHARACTERISTICS	
Buyer-seller similarity	Should we focus on companies whose people and values are similar to ours?
Attitudes toward risk	Should we focus on risk-taking or risk-avoiding customers?
Loyalty	Should we focus on companies that show high loyalty to their suppliers?

Adapted from: Kotler, Philip and Gary Armstrong, *Principles of Marketing*, Tenth Edition.. Upper Saddle River, NJ: Pearson/Prentice Hall, 2004.

Note: For further information go to www.claritas.com. Click on "You Are Where You Live" button.
This site integrates many of the above characteristics into usable profiles based on where you live.

CREATE A 360-DEGREE STRATEGY.

Think of "strategy" as a guide to how you deliver value to your customers. Value is added or subtracted every time your customer interacts with your company. Or every time you "touch" the customer – receptionist's tone of voice, response time, product quality, warranties, value-adds, website, and follow-thru – just to name a few.

Map all the possible touch points customers have with your company.
Now, go build a total strategy around those points – at every step, show how your actions will live up to your mission.

Value Creating Strategy

PURPOSE: To make choices that allow you to match your company's strengths with market opportunities to positively position your company in the mind of your customers.

Think about what a strategy is: It's the process of making trade-offs and choices about how to allocate scarce resources. A company that has infinite resources doesn't need a strategy. Do you know of any company that has infinite resources? — Orit Gadiesh, Chairman, Bain & Co

A value creating strategy is a *directional statement* that serves as a central theme guiding and coordinating integrated actions in the pursuit of a sustainable competitive advantage. Strategy is about having a direction and making choices to move in that direction. Successful companies deliberately make choices to be unique and different in activities that they are really, really good at.

A successful business is about creating value for its customers and the intent or plan should be to create more value than the competitors. A successful value creating strategy matches the company's strengths (resources and capabilities) with market opportunities to create a sustainable competitive advantage by providing more value for its customers than their competitors.

QUESTIONS TO ANSWER:
To determine your strategy, answer these questions:
>   How will you reach these target Customer groups?
>   Will it provide value to your customers in meeting their needs?
>   How will you achieve the targeted results?

TYPES OF VALUE CREATING STRATEGIES:
The basic differences among competitive strategies are:
1. Whether a company's target market is *broad or narrow…and*
2. Whether it is pursuing a competitive advantage based on *low cost efficient operations* or a *particular uniqueness perceived by customers.*

ACTION ITEMS
Choose one of the three basic strategies for each Customer group. Remember: When choosing a strategy, it needs to mesh with your company's strengths and opportunities in the marketplace.

MARKET FOCUS
With a successful strategy, you will provide more value to your customers than your competitors will.

We will be choosing *one strategy* for each of your target *Customer groups*. You should focus on a single strategy for each group; otherwise the danger is you will be mediocre at serving each Customer group. It is acceptable to adopt one strategy for all groups; however it is not wise to adopt two strategies for one group. The "Strategy Comparison Chart" on the next page provides more detail on each strategy. The following are the most basic strategies and typically cover most business operations:

Operational Excellence
This strategy focuses on appealing to a *broad spectrum* of customers based on being the *overall low-cost provider* of a product or service because of the company's *focus on efficiency*. The company provides superior value to their customers by offering them lowest total cost. It works to reduce costs and to create a lean and efficient value-delivery system. It serves customers who want reliable, good-quality products or services, but who want them cheaply and easily.

Product/Service Leadership

This strategy concentrates on creating a *unique, innovative product/service line.* A marketing program is implemented so that a *broad spectrum* of customers perceives the company is offering *leading-edge products or services.* The company provides superior value by offering its customers a continuous stream of innovative products or services. It seeks to identify emerging opportunities and continuously strives to develop and deliver new products and services.

Customer Intimacy

This strategy concentrates on a *narrow market segment* by a *deep understanding of its customer* and their perception of the value of the product or service offered. The company provides superior value by tailoring its products or services to match exactly the needs of targeted customers. It specializes in satisfying unique customer needs through an *intimate* knowledge of them. It builds detailed customer databases for segmenting and targeting, and empowers its marketing people to respond quickly to customer needs.

STRATEGY COMPARISON CHART

Type of Strategy	Operational Excellence – Lower Costs	Product/Service Leadership	Customer Intimacy
Strategic Target	A *broad* cross-section of the market.	Usually a *broad* cross-section of the market where buyers want the newest leading-edge products/ services.	A *narrow* market segment where buyer needs and preferences are distinctively different from the rest of the market.
Basis of Competitive Advantage	Offer buyers lowest total cost because of company's focus on efficiency. This is due to a combination of quality, price, and ease of purchase that is difficult to match.	Offer buyers new and innovative products and services. Perceived as being creative with ideas. Able to leapfrog products that exist. Able to commercialize quickly.	Offer people superior value by tailoring products or services to match exactly the needs of targeted customers due to an intimate knowledge of the customers. Empower people to respond quickly to customer needs.
Sustaining the Strategy	Optimize processes for end-to-end product supply and basic service. Streamline processes to minimize costs & hassle.	Focus on the core processes of invention, product development, and market exploitation.	Focus on a deep understanding of the customer and his perception of value of the product or service offered. Pursue the relationship rather than transaction.
	Maintain standardized, simplified, tightly controlled, and centrally planned operations. Have few decisions for rank and file.	Maintain structure that is flexible to entrepreneurial initiatives. Encourage working in unexplored territory. Promote multifunctional teams to shorten response times.	Empower frontline managers with decision-making authority. Maintain a structure that delegates decision-making to employees who are close to customer.
	Maintain integrated, reliable, and high-speed transactions. Focus on compliance to norms. Generate a culture that abhors waste & rewards efficiency.	Rewards new product success. Encourages imagination, creativity experimentation, accomplishment, out-of-the-box thinking, and risk-taking.	Operations are geared toward nurturing clients. Culture that embraces specific rather than general solutions. Culture that thrives on deep relationships.
Examples	Wal-Mart, Dell, McDonald's, Southwest Airlines, Fed Ex	Sony, Microsoft, Nike, Johnson & Johnson	Amazon, Land's End, Home Depot, Cable & Wireless

Worksheet: Choosing Your Value Creating Strategy

Directions: Use the diagram to help you visualize the different types of strategies. Write down each Customer group in the appropriate area below.

Source of Competitive Advantage

	Cost	Uniqueness
Broad	Operational Excellence	Product/Service Leadership
Narrow	Customer Intimacy	

(vertical axis label: **Breadth of Market**)

Directions: List Constituent/Stakeholder groups. Select one type of strategy for each target Customer group. You may choose the *same* strategy for all groups.

Customer Group: _____   **Value Creating Strategy:** _____

Customer Group: _____   **Value Creating Strategy:** _____

Customer Group: _____   **Value Creating Strategy:** _____

EVALUATION
A value creating strategy leads to a sustainable competitive advantage. The following criteria are to be used as thought-provoking questions. It is not necessary for your strategy to meet all these criteria.

Criteria for Choosing a Value Creating Strategy	☑
Will the strategy create and maintain a competitive advantage through cost based on operational excellence, product/service leadership, or customer intimacy?	
Will the strategy put the business in a position to ward off known threats, exploit opportunities, enhance current advantages, or provide new sources of advantages?	
How difficult will it be for competitors to match or leapfrog the expected advantages?	
Does it build a company reputation and recognizable industry position?	

BEFORE YOU MOVE ON:
Will your business be able to sustain the strategy?

MAKE THAT DECISION.

A decision today is twice as worthy as a decision tomorrow.
There are four reasons people put off making decisions.
1. Not enough data.
2. Too much data.
3. Don't know a decision is required.
4. Afraid of losing their job.

The one thing most executives and managers forget is that the lack of a decision results in more derailments of mission than any other cause.

Goals

PURPOSE: To set goals that convert the company's mission, vision and objectives into specific performance targets.

For change to take hold in an organization, it must be linked explicitly and tightly to real performance goals. - Charles Fishman, Fast Company writer

Goals are immediate mileposts on your way to your vision. Think about achieving them in a one-year timeframe. With goals, the company converts the mission, vision, and strategic objectives into performance targets. Realistic goals ought to serve as a tool for stretching a company to reach its full potential; this means setting them high enough to be challenging to energize the company and its strategy.

A goal is a realistic, measurable, and time-dated target of accomplishment in the future that supports your long-term objectives. Goals move objectives to specifics with respect to *magnitude* and *time*. Goals are something the company's progress can be measured by. Without goals it is impossible for the company to know how it is progressing, who should be reward for progress, and where change is needed.

For effective goals to function as yardsticks for tracking a company's performance and progress, they must state *how much* of *what kind* of performance *by when* it is to be accomplished. They must be relevant, aggressive yet achievable, and be stated in measurable or quantifiable terms. Make them SMART goals based on the criteria below.

QUESTIONS TO ANSWER:
Write specific goals by answering the questions:
What is to be accomplished through your company?
What are your specific, measurable, realistic targets of accomplishment?

CRITERIA:
The following is an explanation of the criteria for SMART goals:

- **Specific**
  Goals must answer the questions: "How much" and "What kind" of performance is to be accomplished?

- **Measurable**
  Goals must be stated in measurable or quantifiable terms or otherwise are only good intentions. Measurable goals facilitate management planning, implementation, and control.

- **Attainable**
  Goals must provide a stretch that inspires people to aim higher. Goals must be aggressive, yet achievable, or they are a set up for failure. Set goals you know you can realistically reach.

- **Relevant**
  Goals must pertain directly to the performance challenge. Goals must maintain consistency and focus. Conflicting goals cause frustration and lack of focus.

ACTION ITEMS
Write your goals in three separate steps.
1. Formulate Financial goals based on each respective objective.
2. Formulate Customer goals based on each respective objective, Customer Group and Value Creating Strategy.
3. Formulate Internal/Operational and People/Learning goals to support the Customer and Financial goals.

MARKET FOCUS
Reflect on the Strengths and Opportunities you identified in your SWOT. When writing goals make sure you capitalize on your strengths and take advantage of your opportunities.

- **Time Specific**
  Goals must answer the question "by when" is it to be accomplished. They must be specific and contain a deadline for achievement.

- **Be in pencil**
  Goals should be in pencil, or they become concrete boxes. They should not be used like whips. Goals are based on today, and they may need to change tomorrow.

It is important for the company to view goals as motivational targets, and exciting, measurable milestones for the future. Your company must decide the time frame that fits your team best. However, it is suggested that you *begin by writing 1-year goals*.

EXAMPLES:
The following are examples of company goals based on the above criteria, which support the objectives. A measurement is stated and a timeframe for accomplishment. Additionally note that the goals have been written in the four major areas. The People/Learning goals provide the basis for the Internal/Operational goals, which support the Customer goals resulting in increased Financial success.

Objective	Goal	Measurement
Financial		
Revenue Growth: To exceed $20 million in the next ten years.	1. To increase our billing hours by 10% in the next 12 months. 2. To achieve a net sales growth of 10% per year.	1. Billable hours compared to last month 2. Net sales compared to last month
Customer		
Customer Retention: Maintain existing customer base by increasing repeat customers.	1. 30% of the company's annual sales must come from products fewer than four years old.	1. Sales on products <4 yrs. old
Internal/Operational		
Operations Management: To continually improve processes to realize efficiencies.	1. To reduce the time lapse between order data and delivery by 2 days by this June. 2. To increase the rate of before or on-time delivery by 5% by June.	1. Order process time 2. Delivery time
Operations Management: To continually improve processes to realize efficiencies.	1. To reduce turnover among sales managers by 10% by the end of the year. 2. To hire and train a human relations director by the end of the year.	1. Manage turnover 2. # of resumes, # of interview, # of finalists
People/Learning		
Knowledge: To continually learn and adopt current best practices.	1. For each principal to attend a best practice conference once a year.	1. # of principals who attended conferences

Worksheet: Writing Goals

With goals, the company converts the mission, vision, and objectives into performance targets. For holistic planning for success, goals will be written for four major areas: Financial, Customer, Internal/ Operational, and People/Learning. Goals must be specific, measurable, aggressive yet achievable, relevant, time specific, and in pencil.

BRAINSTORMING

Directions: Look at the piece of paper where you brainstormed your objectives. Use this brainstorming map to help develop your goals. It is critical to develop goals that support the objectives, which in turn will support your mission and vision.

Worksheet: Goals – Financial

Financial goals support the objectives by focusing on achieving acceptable profitability in a company's pursuit of its mission, vision, long-term health, and ultimate survival.

Directions:
- Write your **Financial Objectives** in the spaces below.
- Under **Goals** write one or more goals that support each objective.
- Under **Measurement** write *how* the goals will be measured and tracked on a monthly basis.

Financial Objective:

Goals	Measurement

Financial Objective:

Goals	Measurement

BEFORE YOU MOVE ON:
Do your Financial goals support your Financial objectives?

Worksheet: Goals – Customer

Customer goals support the objectives. These goals focus on meeting the needs and wants of specific customers through products and services. Thus, you will develop goals based on each Customer group.

Directions:
- Write your **Customer Objectives** and the names of your **Customer Groups** below.
- Under **Goals** write one or more goals based on how you will serve this group.
- Under **Measurement** write *how* the goals will be measured and tracked on a monthly basis.
- When you have completed the goals for all groups, review them together and make sure they support the Customer objectives.

Customer Objective:

Customer Objective:

Customer Objective:

Customer Group:

Goals	Measurement

Customer Group:

Goals	Measurement

Customer Group:

Goals	Measurement

BEFORE YOU MOVE ON:
Do your Customer goals support your Customer objectives and your Financial objectives?

Worksheet: Goals – Internal/Operational

Internal/Operational goals support the objectives by focusing on business processes that have an impact on creating customer value and satisfaction. They focus on maintaining and/or enhancing the company's core competencies. They focus on internal management activities, processes, and operational functions needed to support the Customer goals.

Directions:
▪ Write your **Internal/Operational Objectives** below.
▪ Under **Goals** write one or more goals that support each objective.
▪ Under **Measurement** write *how* the goals will be measured and tracked on a monthly basis.

Internal/Operational Objective:

Goals	Measurement

Internal/Operational Objective:

Goals	Measurement

BEFORE YOU MOVE ON:
Do your Internal/Operational goals support your Internal/Operational objectives and your Customer objectives?

Worksheet: Goals – People/Learning

People/Learning goals support the objectives by focusing on activities that assist to improve and build the company's value creating activities. They focus development of people, increasing the company's knowledge base, continuous improvement through innovation and learning best practices, so that the company is continually on the cutting edge.

Directions:
- Write your **People/Learning Objectives** below.
- Under **Goals** write one or more goals that support each objective.
- Under **Measurement** write *how* the goals will be measured and tracked on a monthly basis.

People/Learning Objective:

Goals	Measurement

People/Learning Objective:

Goals	Measurement

BEFORE YOU MOVE ON:
Do your People/Learning goals support your People/Learning objectives and your Customer objectives?

FOCUS ON THE CONTROL POINTS. LET EVERYTHING ELSE GO.

The temptation is to try to change everything at once. To leap from being the company you are today to the company you want to be—overnight. The fact is you can execute 90 percent of the necessary change by simply pressing on a few carefully chosen control points in your organization. Identify those points and initially put everything else on hold.

Action Items

PURPOSE: Create specific actions that lead to implementing your strategies and achieving your financial and customer goals.

There is always a better way of doing things. Either you or your competitor will find it.
– Brad Anderson, SolArc Inc.

Action Items are specific action/action plans that lead to achieving your short-term goals. They are basically a to-do list for each short-term goal. It involves listing out the concrete steps that you need to accomplish in order to achieve your goals. An action plan explains who is going to do what, by when, and in what order for the organization to reach its goals. The design and implementation of the action planning depend on the nature and needs of the organization.

To ensure implementation of Action Items, it is important to assign responsibilities and deadlines. A great method to get buy-in from your staff is to assign each goal to an individual person or team. Ask him/her to write the action plan and be responsible for making sure each task is accomplished. Another method is to identify all the actions that need to occur in the next 90 days. You can continue this same process every 90 day increment until the goal is achieved.

QUESTIONS TO ANSWER:
A quick way to develop your Action Items is to answer this question:
> What activities need to occur in the next 90 days?
> What roadblocks exist to achieving the goals?

ACTION ITEM AREAS:
You will write Action Items for all the Customer, Internal/Operational, and People/Learning goals. Financial goals do not have Action Items because these goals are the result of achieving the Customer (revenue from customers) and Internal/Operational goals (cost savings from process improvements).

The Action Items for "Customer" are broken down into four areas. This is due to the fact that customers interact with the company in four major areas – product, price, promotion, and place. These four areas provide the framework for creating Action Items to implement your strategies to reach your target Customer group. Each area needs to work together with your value creating strategy to reach your potential customers. Together the Action Items are what your customer sees of your company; therefore they need to be unified.

QUESTIONS IN THE "CUSTOMER" AREA:
When formulating Action Items for each strategy, the following are the four areas you need to consider:

Product - Customer Solution
The product/service you are offering to your Customer group.
A product/service offering is anything that can be brought to the market, which will provide satisfaction. An offering includes

---

ACTION ITEMS
1. Customer goals: Each Value Creating Strategy has general considerations for formulating your Action Items. Based on the strategy you selected for each Customer group, use the corresponding worksheet to write Action Items to support your goals.
2. Internal/Operational goals: Write Action Items to support these goals.
3. People/Learning goals: Write Action Items to support these goals.

MARKET FOCUS
There are four areas your customers come into contact with your company. Look at each area through their eyes. Based on this information, how should you respond?

---

physical objects, services, events, persons, places, organizations, ideas, and any combination of these.

- What is your customer "really buying" when he/she acquires your product/service?
- What are the benefits the product/service will provide to your customer?
- What are your actual product/service characteristics (quality, features, design, brand name, and packaging) that your customer is "really buying"?
- What are the additional customer services and benefits provided to your customer?
- Is the product under-designed to save production costs?
- Are all features included that the customer needs?

Price - Customer Cost
The amount of money customers have to pay to obtain your product/service. Price is one of the major factors affecting buyer choice and needs to be cohesive with the strategy you picked. Price is the only element of the four Action Item areas that produces revenues as the other areas represent cost areas. Prices need to be set somewhere between product costs and market demand. There are both internal and external factors to consider when setting prices.

- What are your financial objectives and associated goals? How will they be reached?
- Based on the benefits you are providing your customer, what is the perceived value of your product/service?
- What are your "production" costs or minimum amount you need to charge to cover your costs?
- Based on your SWOT, what is the nature of the market demand? How much can you charge for your product/service without pricing yourself out of the market?
- How price-sensitive are your customers?
- Will prices be consistent throughout the Customer group?

Promotion - Communication
The activities that communicate the benefits of the product/service and persuade your potential customers to buy. Customers do not distinguish between messages about a company and its products/ services. Thus the necessity to manage the total promotional program and ensure it is *sending a unified consistent message.* This idea is called "integrated marketing communications." To deliver the message, a mix of the following well-known communication tools is used: advertising, direct marketing, sales promotion, public relations, and personal selling.

- What is the message you need to communicate to your customers?
- What are the best communication tools you can use to reach your customer?
- What sales material do you need to have to sell your product/service?
- How will promotion support your financial objectives and supporting goals?
- What internal activities do you need to look at to be communicating a unified message?
- Are all messages honestly communicating the value of the products/services?

Place (Distribution) - Channel
The company's activities that make the product/service available to target customers. The channel is a conduit for bringing together a company and its customers at some place and time in order to appropriately serve them. The channel makes the product/service available to the customers. In order to obtain the product/service it needs to be convenient, personally pleasant, and rewarding. People in your distribution channels in many instances provide greater efficiency in making goods and services available to your target markets because of contacts, experience, specialization, and scale of operation.

- How do your customers expect to find your product/service?
- Who else (if anyone) is involved in bringing your product/service to your customers?
- What costs need to be considered for the different channel options?
- Does your product/service have any unique characteristics that might affect distribution?
- Are all incentives provided in the distribution channels ethical and appropriate?

Worksheet: Action Items – Customer

Each Value Creating Strategy (see Step 8) is presented on separate pages. Select **one strategy** for each Customer group. Based on the Value Creating Strategy, a list of tactical considerations is provided for implementation. The listed tactics support the particular strategy. They will guide you in creating Action Items for implementing your selected strategy and achieving your goals.
Directions:
1. Under the selected *Value Creating Strategy*, list the targeted *Customer group* and associated *Goals* written in the previous step.
2. Write *Action Items* for each Customer area – product, price, promotion, and distribution. Make sure your Action Items support your Customer Goals for the Customer group.
3. For each *Action Items* assign the *Person Responsible*. Include a *Deadline* to ensure implementation.

Strategy: **Operational Excellence**

Customer Group:

Goals

	Product/Customer Solution		
Tactic	*How will you implement this tactic?* *Action Items*	*Person Responsible*	*Deadline*
A good basic hassle-free product/service offering with limited selection but solid value.			

	Price/Customer Costs		
Tactic	*How will you implement this tactic?* *Action Items*	*Person Responsible*	*Deadline*
Low cost relative to competitors. Low price due to design, production, operations, scale of economies, or experience.			

	Promotion /Communication		
Tactic	*How will you implement this tactic?* *Action Items*	*Person Responsible*	*Deadline*
Emphasizes value for the customer due to a "fine tuned" system and process.			

	Distribution/Channel		
Tactic	*How will you implement this tactic?* *Action Items*	*Person Responsible*	*Deadline*
Well-developed channel of distribution providing no-hassle service. Logistics are a key.			

Worksheet: Action Items – Customer

Based on the below Value Creating Strategy, a list of tactical considerations is provided for implementing this strategy. The listed tactics are the most likely scenarios necessary to support the particular strategy. They will guide you in creating Action Items for implementing your strategy and achieving your goals.

Directions:
1. Under the selected Value Creating Strategy, list the targeted *Customer group* and associated *Goals* written in the previous step.
2. Write *Action Items* for each Customer area – product, price, promotion, and distribution. Make sure your Action Items support your Customer Goals for the Customer group.
3. For *Action Items* assign the *Person Responsible*. Include a *Deadline* to ensure implementation.

Strategy: **Product/Service Leadership**

Customer Group:

Goals

Product/Customer Solution			
Tactic	*How will you implement this tactic?* *Action Items*	*Person Responsible*	*Deadline*
Products/services that push performance boundaries. A continual stream of enhancements or new products.			

Price/Customer Costs			
Tactic	*How will you implement this tactic?* *Action Items*	*Person Responsible*	*Deadline*
Higher than "normal" price because it is a state-of-the art product/service. Price supports the uniqueness and timeliness of the product/service.			

Promotion/Communication			
Tactic	*How will you implement this tactic?* *Action Items*	*Person Responsible*	*Deadline*
Emphasizes product/service performance and innovation perspective.			

Distribution/Channel			
Tactic	*How will you implement this tactic?* *Action Items*	*Person Responsible*	*Deadline*
Channels are fast reacting and supportive.			

Worksheet: Action Items – Customer

Based on the below Value Creating Strategy, a list of tactical considerations is provided for implementing this strategy. The listed tactics are the most likely scenarios necessary to support the particular strategy. They will guide you in creating Action Items for implementing your strategy and achieving your goals.

Directions:
1. Under the selected Value Creating Strategy, list the targeted *Customer group* and associated *Goals* written in the previous step.
2. Write *Action Items* for each Customer area – product, price, promotion, and distribution. Make sure your Action Items support your Customer Goals for the Customer group.
3. For *Action Items* assign the *Person Responsible*. Include a *Deadline* to ensure implementation.

Strategy:	**Customer Intimacy**
Customer Group:	
Goals	

Product/Customer Solution			
Tactic	How will you implement this tactic? *Action Items*	*Person Responsible*	*Deadline*
A product/service based on what a customer needs, rather than what the market wants. It provides solutions/advice to assist customer solving problem or fulfilling a unique need.			

Price/Customer Costs			
Tactic	How will you implement this tactic? *Action Items*	*Person Responsible*	*Deadline*
Reasonable price cultivates long-term relationships and loyalty. Customer gets more than expected. Price focuses on customer lifetime value.			

Promotion/Communication			
Tactic	How will you implement this tactic? *Action Items*	*Person Responsible*	*Deadline*
Emphasizes the best solution for buyer while achieving optimum results. Emphasizes understanding customer and his perception of value.			

Distribution/Channel			
Tactic	How will you implement this tactic? *Action Items*	*Person Responsible*	*Deadline*
Complete support and solutions. Understands needs of the customer.			

Worksheet: Action Items – Internal/Operational

Directions:
1. Write *Action Items* to support your Internal/Operational Goals written in the previous step.
2. Assign the *Person Responsible*.
3. Determine a *Deadline* to ensure implementation.

Internal/Operational Objective:			
Goals	Action Items	Person Responsible	Deadline

Internal/Operational Objective:			
Goals	Action Items	Person Responsible	Deadline

Internal/Operational Objective:			
Goals	Action Items	Person Responsible	Deadline

Internal/Operational Objective:			
Goals	Action Items	Person Responsible	Deadline

Worksheet: Action Items – People/Learning

Directions:
1. Write *Action Items* to support your People/Learning Goals written in the previous step.
2. Assign the *Person Responsible*.
3. Determine a *Deadline* to ensure implementation.

People/Learning Objective:			
Goals	Action Items	Person Responsible	Deadline

People/Learning Objective:			
Goals	Action Items	Person Responsible	Deadline

People/Learning Objective:			
Goals	Action Items	Person Responsible	Deadline

People/Learning Objective:			
Goals	Action Items	Person Responsible	Deadline

BEFORE YOU MOVE ON:
Are all Goals adequately supported by Action Items?

LET THE NUMBERS TELL THE STORY.

Figures don't lie, but liars figure.

The financials will tell you what goals to keep and what to cut.
Keep the goals with a positive story. Revised the ones with a negative ending.
After all, we all like a story with a happy ending.

Financial Assessment

PURPOSE: To assess the expenses and potential revenue associated with implementing your plan.

You don't get points for intent, only for results. – Annie Morita, Columbia TriStar

Now that you have completed your goals and action items for each Customer group, it is time to develop a Financial Assessment. While your action items and goals are top of mind, you need to put some estimated costs associated with implementing each item. One of the biggest stumbling blocks to all well laid strategic plans is time and money. In this step we will look at not only the estimated expenses, but also the potential revenue. This will help you make decisions about when to implement certain action items and if your cash outlay will generate the required revenue to meet your financial goals. As with every business, budgets are never big enough to do everything you want to do.

QUESTIONS TO ANSWER:
Prioritize key goals by asking:
> Does implementing the goals to target this Customer group make financial sense?
> Do you have the human resources to achieve your plan?

ASSESSMENT PROCESS:
For each strategy targeting a Customer group, do the following:
1. Look at your Action Items and note those that have related expenses.
2. Estimate expenses for each Action Item, focusing on large expense centers.
3. Estimate revenue expected for each group.
4. Develop a profit/loss analysis that looks at direct costs and revenues.
5. Assess what is to be accomplished with what you can realistically afford.
6. Prioritize your goals and action items.

> ### ACTION ITEMS
> 1. Identify strategies or goals that have related expenses.
> 2. Estimate expenses for executing each strategy.
> 3. Estimate revenue expected.
> 4. Develop a contribution analysis.
> 5. Determine priorities for each area of the plan.
>
> ### MARKET FOCUS
> Implementing some Action Items may be direct revenue generators of your strategic plan.

Note: You will first do a financial assessment for each Customer group. This will be followed by an assessment of your Internal/Operational and People/Learning action items. If you decide to execute Strategy A to reach Customer group X, make sure you have funded any Internal/Operational and People/Learning Goals that support this strategy. Finally all of this information will be incorporated into a budget.

ESTIMATING EXPENSES & REVENUES:
Expense and revenue estimating is an imperfect science. However, it is meant to give you a general idea of the additional cash outlay required to implement each area of your plan, and the revenue you can expect to generate. The worksheets that follow provide you with an area to list potential expense and revenue centers for goals and/or strategies. It is important to identify large expenses that might prohibit implementation.

This overall process provides management with a perspective that is externally focused on the Customer groups they serve. Use the worksheets on the following pages to estimate whether your selected strategy and action items may be successful.

Worksheet: Financial Assessment – Explanation

Directions: Identify each Customer group.
In this step it will be necessary for you to develop credible estimates for the Revenue and related Expenses for each Customer group. Estimates are never easy to develop, but credible estimates provide the basis for good managerial decisions. So do your homework!

Customer Group:

Estimated Revenue

Directions: What is the estimated revenue for this Customer group?
Refer back to the *Worksheet: Targeting Your Customer Group* in Step 7.There are a number of methods to develop an estimate, and this is only one.
▪   Estimated number of customers:_____
▪   Estimated average sale per customer: _____   (Based on your *Price* Tactic developed in Step 10.)
      (If there is a significant difference between old and new customers, take this into consideration.)
▪   Estimated number of sales per customer per year: _____
▪   **Estimated Revenue this Year = _____**
      (Number of customers x average sale per customer x number of sales per customer per year)

Contribution Analysis

Directions: Develop a Contribution Analysis by estimating Revenues and Costs per quarter for one year. A Contribution Analysis provides you with a projection of whether your strategy will generate revenues in excess of expenses. If the Contribution Analysis determines that the dollar investment in the strategy to reach this Customer group cannot be justified, a rethinking and adjustment of Customer and Financial goals is needed. Once adjusted, determine if the new strategy will meet payback expectations.

	Explanation
Estimated Revenue	Based on your Estimated Revenue calculations this year.
<Cost of Goods Sold>	Based on your *Product Tactic* developed in Step 10 that established the Unit Cost. Cost of Goods Sold = Unit Cost x number of sales per customer per year
Gross Margin	Subtract Cost of Goods Sold from Estimated Revenue
<Additional Overhead Costs>	Based on your *Promotion Tactic* and *Distribution Tactic* developed in Step 10, you may have associated expenses for this Customer group. These Overhead Costs will be subtracted from the Gross Margin.
<Additional Managerial Costs>	You may have *Internal/Operational* expenses * required to target this Customer group. These additional Managerial Costs will be subtracted from the Gross Margin.
	You may have *People/Learning* expenses * required to target this Customer group. These additional Managerial Costs will be subtracted from the Gross Margin.
Contribution to Operations	

* These are calculated in the following worksheets.

Worksheet: Financial Assessment – Customer

Directions: Identify each Customer group. Based on your strategy to reach this Customer group, estimate Revenue and Expenses. Then develop a Contribution Analysis.

Customer Group:

Estimated Revenue

Directions: What is the estimated revenue for this Customer group?
Refer back to the *Worksheet: Targeting Your Customer Group* in Step 7. There are a number of methods to develop an estimate, and this is only one.

- Estimated number of customers:_____
- Estimated average sale per customer: _____ (Based on your *Price Tactic* developed in Step 10.)
  (If there is a significant difference between old and new customers, take this into consideration.)
- Estimated number of sales per customer per year: _____
- **Estimated Revenue this Year** = _____
  (Number of customers x average sale per customer x number of sales per customer per year)

Estimate Expenses

Directions: Based on your strategy to reach this Customer group, review your tactical Actions Items in Step 10. List those that have expenses. Estimate expenses for one year.

Action Items	Amount
Product	
Promotion	
Distribution	

Contribution Analysis

Directions: Develop a Contribution Analysis by estimating Revenues and Costs for this year.
Is this group profitable? Estimated Revenue – Estimated Expenses = Profit

	Quarter One	Quarter Two	Quarter Three	Quarter Four	Total
Estimated Revenue					
<Cost of Goods Sold>					
Gross Margin					
<Additional Overhead Costs>					
<Additional Managerial Costs>					
Contribution to Operations					

BEFORE YOU MOVE ON: Does targeting this Customer group make financial sense? Does the company have the right skills and resources? Yes☐   No☐

Worksheet: Financial Assessment – Customer

Directions: Identify each Customer group. Based on your strategy to reach this Customer group, estimate Revenue and Expenses. Then develop a Contribution Analysis.

Customer Group:

Estimated Revenue

Directions: What is the estimated revenue for this Customer group?
Refer back to the *Worksheet: Targeting Your Customer Group* in Step 7. There are a number of methods to develop an estimate, and this is only one.

- Estimated number of customers:_____
- Estimated average sale per customer: _____ (Based on your *Price Tactic* developed in Step 10.)
    (If there is a significant difference between old and new customers, take this into consideration.)
- Estimated number of sales per customer per year: _____
- **Estimated Revenue this Year** = _____
    (Number of customers x average sale per customer x number of sales per customer per year)

Estimate Expenses

Directions: Based on your strategy to reach this Customer group, review your tactical Actions Items in Step 10. List those that have expenses. Estimate expenses for one year.

Action Items	Amount
Product	
Promotion	
Distribution	

Contribution Analysis

Directions: Develop a Contribution Analysis by estimating Revenues and Costs for this year.
Is this group profitable? Estimated Revenue – Estimated Expenses = Profit

	Quarter One	Quarter Two	Quarter Three	Quarter Four	Total
Estimated Revenue					
<Cost of Goods Sold>					
Gross Margin					
<Additional Overhead Costs>					
<Additional Managerial Costs>					
Contribution to Operations					

BEFORE YOU MOVE ON: Does targeting this Customer group make financial sense? Does the company have the right skills and resources? Yes☐ No☐

Worksheet: Financial Assessment – Customer

Directions: Identify each Customer group. Based on your strategy to reach this Customer group, estimate Revenue and Expenses. Then develop a Contribution Analysis.

Customer Group:

Estimated Revenue

Directions: What is the estimated revenue for this Customer group?
Refer back to the *Worksheet: Targeting Your Customer Group* in Step 7. There are a number of methods to develop an estimate, and this is only one.

- Estimated number of customers:_____
- Estimated average sale per customer: _____ (Based on your *Price Tactic* developed in Step 10.)
   (If there is a significant difference between old and new customers, take this into consideration.)
- Estimated number of sales per customer per year: _____
- **Estimated Revenue this Year = _____**
   (Number of customers x average sale per customer x number of sales per customer per year)

Estimate Expenses

Directions: Based on your strategy to reach this Customer group, review your tactical Actions Items in Step 10. List those that have expenses. Estimate expenses for one year.

Action Items	Amount
Product	
Promotion	
Distribution	

Contribution Analysis

Directions: Develop a Contribution Analysis by estimating Revenues and Costs for this year.
Is this group profitable? Estimated Revenue – Estimated Expenses = Profit

	Quarter One	Quarter Two	Quarter Three	Quarter Four	Total
Estimated Revenue					
<Cost of Goods Sold>					
Gross Margin					
<Additional Overhead Costs>					
<Additional Managerial Costs>					
Contribution to Operations					

BEFORE YOU MOVE ON: Does targeting this Customer group make financial sense? Does the company have the right skills and resources? Yes☐ No☐

Worksheet: Financial Assessment – Internal/Operational

Directions: Based on your Internal/Operational goals, review your *Action Items* in Step 10 and enter estimated expenses for each item. Estimate expenses for one year.
These expenses are entered as "Additional Managerial Costs" in the Contribution Analysis.

Expense Estimating

Action Items	Amount

Worksheet: Financial Assessment – People/Learning

Directions: Based on your People/Learning goals, review your *Action Items* in Step 10 and enter estimated expenses for each item. Estimate expenses for one year.
These expenses are entered as "Additional Managerial Costs" in the Contribution Analysis.

Expense Estimating

Action Items	Amount

Organizational Budget

In conjunction with assessment of the required *Action Items*, a budget should be developed to encapsulate all information. Most operational actions are not stand alone activities and must be analyzed within the framework of the total organization.

Fiscal Year Ending _____

REVENUE	Amount	Amount
Source		
	$	
Total Revenue		$
EXPENDITURES		
Action Items (Internal/Operational) – unapplied		$
Action Items (People/Learning) – unapplied		$
Payroll		
Salaries	$	
Hourly Wages		
Taxes (social security, unemployment, state, etc)		
Benefits (health, life, pension, etc.)		
Other		
Total Payroll Expenditures		$
Occupancy		
Rent or Gross Mortgage Payments	$	
Insurance		
Cleaning		
Utilities		
Other		
Total Occupancy Expenditures		$
Operations		
Professional Fees		
Equipment Rental		
Office Supplies		
Repairs		
Telephone		
Copying		
Promotion		
Other		
Total Operations Expenditures		$
Cash Flow from Revenue		$
Capital Expenditures	$	
Capital Expenditures		
Total Capital Expenditures		$
REVENUES in excess of EXPENDITURES		$

SINGLE OUT THE KEY FACTORS THAT DRIVE YOUR SUCCESS.

You can't monitor everything in your organization.
But you can focus on a few key indicators.
Single out the two or three factors that focus on your mission.
Watch them daily.
Track them weekly.
Evaluate them monthly.
Take corrective action promptly.

Strategic Scorecard

PURPOSE: To measure and manage your strategic plan.

You cannot manage what you cannot measure…And what gets measured gets done. —Bill Hewlett

To help measure and manage your Strategic Plan, we have modified the concepts from two Harvard professors and consultants – Kaplan and Norton. They devised a tool, the Balanced Scorecard, which provides the framework for comprehensive performance measurement. For our purposes, we have simplified the Balanced Scorecard and are calling it a *Strategic Scorecard*. It incorporates traditional financial measures, which are focused on short-term results and internal activities, with non-financial measures that are focused on future oriented activities, as well as external or market activities.

Keep in mind that the Strategic Scorecard is to be used as both a measurement and management tool to assist in fulfilling your company's vision. Think of it as an instrument panel guiding your company toward achieving an integrated single strategy. With it, you can actively track progress towards your goals. You can use it to make your company more strategy-focused and deliver demonstrable performance that is aligned with your vision and mission.

QUESTIONS TO ANSWER

One of the keys in developing the appropriate measurements is to have a clear and easy to understand strategy. Answers to the following questions will help you identify measurements:

    What does the company really do?
    What are the key success measures for your organization?
    What value do your activities provide for your customers?
    What are the outcomes of these activities?

> **ACTION ITEMS**
> Develop a set of outcome measures to help manage and monitor your goals. Set targets to achieve the goals. Remember: Measures are unique to your company.
>
> **MARKET FOCUS**
> Developing outcome measures and action items to manage your current market is critical for long-term success. It is also important to monitor new market opportunities.

TYPES OF MEASUREMENT AND TARGETS:

The Strategic Scorecard has two types of measurements – a primary *outcome measure* that is associated with a goal and a secondary *action item*. These two types of measures report a cause and effect. The action items actually work towards the accomplishment of goals which have outcome measures. The Action Items and Short-term Goals have been previously developed in Steps Nine and Ten. They are being brought together in this step.

- **Outcome Measures & Targets:** These items describe how a goal is to be tracked. The *measure* is an explanation (word text) of what you want to achieve. The *target* is a numeric description or specific number of the precise amount of the measure you need to hit in order to achieve your goal and can be expressed in weekly, monthly or annual figures. Together these indicate whether the overall strategy has been accomplished. They are an end point.

- **Action Items:** These communicate how the goals are to be achieved. These are the cause or lead items on the path to accomplishing the end result. These are the "to do" items that must be done to hit the goal. When they are measured, they provide a current indicator as to whether the strategy is being implemented.

MEASUREMENT CATEGORIES:

The Strategic Scorecard has four categories of measures. These categories are interconnected with one category impacting the next. They are more fully described in *Strategic Objectives* (Step Five). The process is as follows:

- *People/Learning* represents the efforts to provide an environment for management and staff to learn and grow thus providing enhanced value to the company and the individuals served.

- *Internal/Operational* represents the processes and infrastructure needed for the management and staff to perform their value-producing tasks.

- *Customer* represents how individuals are being served through a value-producing process utilizing an improved infrastructure with committed and energized staff.

- *Financial* represents the end result if the previous categories/activities are working harmoniously.

EXAMPLES OF MEASURES:

The following examples are based on the goals developed in Step Nine for each of the four categories. Specific measures and targets should be developed for your organization's value-creating activities. Best practice organizations tend to manage their operations with as few as 15 measures to possibly 35 or 40. An example of a Strategic Scorecard for a fictitious café is presented after the four categories.

Financial — How will we look to our stakeholders?

Financial measures indicate whether your company's strategy, implementation, and execution are contributing to bottom line and top line improvement. There are no action items for Financial goals, because as previously stated financial outcomes are the result of the three underlying categories being successfully implemented.

Goal	Measure	Target	Action Items
To increase the billing hours by 10% in the next 12 months.	Billable hours compared to last month.	1500 billable hours per month.	No action items for Financial goals.
To achieve a net sales growth of 10% this year.	Net sales compared to last month.	$250,000 of net sales per month.	

Customer — How do we provide value to our customers?

Customer measures and targets are customized to each of your targeted Customer groups from which your company expects growth and profitability. The action items measure and direct your actual progress in providing appropriate value to the targeted groups.

Goal	Measure	Target	Action Items
30% of the company's annual sales must come from products fewer than four years old.	Net sales of products less than 4 years old.	$75,000 of net sales per month.	• Conduct a focus group with 2 largest customer groups regarding product usage within 2 months. • Data mine for purchasing habits of customers buying newer products.

Internal/Operational — To satisfy our customers, what processes must we excel at?
Internal Process measures and targets identify your most critical internal programs and activities in which your company must excel. The measures focus on business processes that have the greatest impact on customer satisfaction, processes that achieve your company's financial objective, and processes based on your core competencies that are needed to sustain your competitive advantage.

Goal	Measure	Target	Action Items
To reduce the time lapse between order date and delivery by 2 days this June.	Order process time.	3 days from order to shipping.	• Improve order taking system of call center by April 30. • Explore improved training for call center by April 30
To increase the rate of before or on-time delivery by 5% by June.	Delivery time.	3 days from shipping to customer receipt.	• Explore UPC coding for all shipments by April 15. • Interview 2 new carriers by March 31.

People/Learning — To excel at our processes, how must we learn and improve?
People/Learning measures and targets identify the infrastructure that your company must build to create long-term growth and improvement. Your ability to attract essential staff, innovate, improve and learn ties directly to your company's value.

Goal	Measure	Target	Action Items
For each principal to attend a best practice conference once a year.	# of principals who attended conference	7 principals	1. Obtain a list of industry-specific conferences by January 1. 2. Solicit principal vacation schedules to compare with available conferences before February 15.

STRATEGIC SCORECARD EXAMPLE: CAFÉ SOLÁ

Short-Term Goal	Measure (explanation)	Targets (numeric)	Action Items
Financial – *How will we look to our stakeholders?*			
Increase ROI from 10% to 15% within the next 12 months.	Revenue growth.	2% to 5% revenue growth.	
	Contribution margin for food and alcohol.	Contribution margin increase of food =1% and alcohol = 2.5%.	
Customer – *How do we provide value to our customers?*			
Increase customer satisfaction with food.	Customer satisfaction survey for food.	8% increase in customer satisfaction.	Monthly focus groups to discuss food quality and variety. Involve them in menu changes.
Increase overall customer loyalty.	Retention rate, not just intention to return.	2% increase in customer loyalty or XX number of repeat customers per month.	Reduction in number of bad experiences of customers.
Internal/Operational – *To satisfy our customers, what processes must we excel at?*			
Increase quality and variety of food items on menu.	Average food ticket.	5% increase in average food ticket.	Addition of two improved or new food items per month.
Reduce time to serve and less wait staff errors.	On a random basis per shift monitor food service.	2 minutes from kitchen to customer (where reasonable).	Weekly training for serving skills of only 15 minutes. Input from staff to be included.
People/Learning – *To excel at our processes, how must we learn and improve?*			
Develop skills in food preparation and service.	Variable Food costs.	2% decrease in expenses annually.	Line chefs' attendance at culinary school by June 30.
Improve servers' knowledge of menu offerings.	Number of food menu tickets per shift.	3 bonuses provided per month based upon 5% increase in # of menu tickets.	Monthly instructional sessions to discuss and explain menu.
Enhance servers' personal skills.	Employee satisfaction.	10 less employee complaints per month.	Quarterly training sessions on interpersonal skills.

Worksheet: Strategic Scorecard

Directions: Finalize your scorecard based on the goals and measurements developed earlier.

Short-Term Goal	Measure (explanation)	Targets (numeric)	Action Items
Financial – *How will we look to our stakeholders?*			
Customers – *How do we provide value to our customers?*			
Internal/Operational – *To satisfy our customers, what processes must we excel at?*			
People/Learning – *To excel at our processes, how must we learn and improve?*			

MAKE EVERYONE A HOLDER OF THE CODE.

Everyone must know the game plan and
Be clear on the direction.
Everyone must understand how they fit in and
How to contribute.

To achieve your vision.

Implementation

PURPOSE: To execute your strategic plan.

Strategies are intellectually simple; their execution is not. – Lawrence Bossidy, CEO Allied-Signal
Just being able to conceive bold new strategies is not enough. The general manager must also be able to translate his or her strategic vision into concrete steps that "get things done." – Richard Hamermesh

A strategic plan will provide a business with the roadmap it needs to pursue a specific strategic direction and set of performance goals, deliver customer value, and be successful. However, this is just a plan; it does not guarantee that the desired performance will be reached any more than having a roadmap guarantees the traveler will arrive at the desired destination. However, the more complete and purposeful the implementation, the more successful the company will be in the marketplace.

To achieve business goals and objectives, a business needs not only a good strategic plan, but also a well-executed implementation of the plan. Implementation is the process that turns strategies and plans into actions in order to accomplish strategic objectives and goals. Whereas the strategic plan addresses the *what* and *why* of activities, implementation addresses the *who, where, when, and how*. It is believed that implementation is as important, or even more important, than strategy. The fact is that both are critical to success. In fact, companies can gain competitive advantage through implementation if done effectively.

FACTS:
According to a cover story in *Fortune* magazine, nine out of ten organizations fail to implement their strategic plan due to the fact that:
- 60% of organizations do not link strategy to budgeting
- 75% of organizations do not link middle management incentives to strategy
- 86% of executive teams spend less than one hour per month discussing strategy
- 95% of a typical workforce does not understand their organization's strategy

QUESTIONS TO ANSWER:
Consider your answers to the following questions for successful implementation of your plan:

How committed are you to implementing the plan to move your company forward?
How will you communicate the plan throughout the company?
Are there sufficient people that will buy-in to drive the plan forward?
Do you have the right people on your team?
How are you going to motivate your people?
Have you identified internal processes that are key to drive the plan forward?
Will you commit money, resources, and time to support the plan?
What are the roadblocks to implementing and supporting the plan?
How will you take available resources and achieve maximum results with them?

ACTION ITEMS
1. Complete the worksheet "Implementing the Strategic Plan."
2. Assign a Strategic Leader needs to monitor the plan.
3. Assign a "Group Leader" to each Customer Group. He/she is responsible for executing the Value Creating Strategy and monitoring the measurement and action items that this strategy affects.
4. The Group Leader selects "Team Members" to develop and complete the action items.
5. List three actions you will take this week to get the plan started.

MARKET FOCUS
You are the Strategic Leader. It is your responsibility to keep all activities and resources aligned with the Strategic Plan.

MAJOR FACTORS:
There are three major areas that contribute to the successful implementation of a strategic plan:

Owning the Plan
- Leader and/or Ownership Team – A leader devoted to the successful implementation of the strategy and plan is critical. Better yet is the creation of an ownership team, who can leverage the unique talents of multiple people and exert organizational influence.

Supporting the Plan
- People – The right people on your team with the required competencies and skills are needed to support the company's competitive advantage.
- Resources – Sufficient personnel, money and time allocated to support implementation are required.
- Structure – Appropriate lines of authority, communication and a mechanism to accomplish the plan is needed.
- Systems – Appropriate management systems empowering and managing people is critical for implementation.
- Culture – An environment that connects employees to the organization's market-focused mission.

Adapting the Plan
- The strategic plan needs to be adaptive to survive changing or unanticipated conditions. Corrective actions need to be taken based on Strategic Scorecard measurements and continuous improvement.

A good strategic plan and implementation effort will enable your business to achieve a market success well beyond planned performance, and in a much shorter time than expected. No one factor presented will make or break the successful implementation of the strategic plan. However, when the sum of these factors is adequately addressed, the chances for successful implementation are greatly improved.

IDEAS FOR SUCCESSFUL IMPLEMENTATION:
The best plan is only a plan, a set of good intentions, unless there is communication, action, appraisal, and continuous reallocation of the company's resources to achieving results. The following are ideas:

Depending on the size of your organization…
- Communicate the strategy to everyone in your organization through the visual Strategy Map provided in the book or at www.onstrategyhq.com.
- Implement your plan using OnStrategy outputs: Full Strategic Plan, Executive Summary, Strategic Map, One-Page Plan, SWOT, Scorecard, One-Click Report and Action Sheets provided at www.onstrategyhq.com.
- Involve your staff in the final development of the plan.
- Have your staff create the action items to support their assigned goals.
- Hold your staff responsible for the achievement of assigned goals.
- Provide frequent and open opportunities to review team and individual performance.
- Monitor the Strategic Scorecard monthly or quarterly. Involve people at all levels of the organization. Give leadership the ability to quickly take corrective action or move to build on success.
- If an action is not working try to improve the strategy, change it, and make another major effort.
- Hold a monthly meeting, one-on-one with the team leaders, where you only discuss strategy.
- Hold a monthly or quarterly staff strategy meeting to report on the progress.
- Re-visit and refine the Strategic Plan three months from now.
- Plan quarterly meetings where you only discuss strategy.
- Give recognition where it is due. Appraisal should focus on achievement. Reward effectiveness.
- Hold yourself accountable through a mentor or personal coach.
- Make true self-assessment an ongoing practice. It is the foundation of excellence in performance.
- Throw a party when goals are reached. Celebrate!

Worksheet: Implementing the Strategic Plan

Directions: There are three major areas that contribute to the successful implementation of a strategic plan: "Owning the Plan," "Supporting the Plan," and "Adapting the Plan". Under each of these areas, consider your answers to the following questions for successful implementation of the plan:

OWNING THE PLAN

The most common reason a plan fails is lack of ownership. If people do not have an ownership stake and responsibility in the plan, it will be business as usual for all but a frustrated few. Ownership of a plan can be enhanced with detailed action plans, a champion leader or ownership team, and chairperson of the board/top management involvement.

Detailed Action Plan: For each Action Item specified, an individual is assigned a specific responsibility, a measurement is delineated, and a time frame within which the action item should be completed is agreed upon. Check to be sure this has been done.   ☑

Champion Leader or Ownership Team: What is the name of the overall Strategic Plan Leader or Team Members who will oversee and champion the successful implementation of the Strategic Plan to move the company forward?

Leader for each Customer group: What is the name of the Group Leader for each Customer group?

Customer Group Name	Group Leader

Communicate the Plan: How will you communicate the plan throughout your company?

Accountability: What is the name of a mentor, personal coach, or business organization that you could hold yourself accountable to for successfully implementing the plan?

Implementation Items: What specific items will you do to implement the plan in the next 90 days?

Monthly Update: What dates will you meet to focus on strategy? What will you do on a monthly basis to make sure your plan is being implemented?

SUPPORTING THE PLAN

The support of a Strategic Plan is influenced by five key components: People, Resources, Structure, Systems, and Culture. All those components must be in sync with each other and with the business in order to support the plan.

People: Do you have the right people on your team with the required competencies and skills? What are the required competencies and skills needed by people at all levels to implement the plan? List any key competencies and skills you still need on your team.

Resources: What personnel, money and time have you directly committed to support the plan?
Personnel:

Money:

Time:

Structure: Do you have the required structural capabilities to support the plan? Do the people and systems fit the structure? Does the structure fit the culture? Write down your thoughts about organizational structure, alliances and networks that are needed.

Systems: Write down your thoughts on internal process systems that are key to drive the plan forward?

Communication Systems: How can you improve organizational communication and effectiveness as it pertains to implementing your strategy? How can you effectively use the visual One-Page Strategic Map to communicate the plan?

Information Systems: Do your personnel have all the information they need to effectively implement the strategy? Is customer information readily accessible to service personnel? Do salespeople have the proper promotional material to present the strategy effectively?

Planning System: How often and when will you hold meetings where you only discuss strategy?

Compensation System: What rewards and incentives will you incorporate to motive your people to support the plan?

Corporate Culture: Organizational culture can be defined as the core beliefs and values that have a high degree of persistence. These intangible factors extend a broad and deep influence on personnel's behavior. Company owners and leaders influence the culture through what they measure, reward, and how they react to situations. How will you connect employees to the company's market-focused mission? How will you motivate their creativity, commitment and passion to the organization?

ADAPTING THE PLAN

Strategic planning is a dynamic process of identifying outcome gaps in relation to the company's vision. If the business is failing to meet its mission, then corrective action must be developed and implemented to ensure that the company is doing what it was formed to do. An important part of strategic planning is always monitoring and adapting the plan to survive changing and/or unanticipated conditions. Factors that contribute to the adaptive nature of the plan are: persistence, continuous improvement and corrective actions based on your feedback metrics.

Persistence: Are you committed to being persistent in adapting the Strategic Plan? ☑

Continuous Improvement: This involves evaluating the results of strategies and plans and taking corrective action to ensure that goals are attained. Once your company has a clear understanding of what it wants to achieve, what it will hold itself accountable for, and what it will cost, then decisions can accurately be made. When decisions must be made, ask, "What will further the mission?" Then take corrective actions on how to allocate time, money, and staff.

Corrective Action: Assess what is happening with your plan.
1. Review the Targets you set in the Strategic Scorecard.
2. Evaluate your performance to date for each Target.
   Mark your progress for each Target as follow:
   Green: We are at or above our target.
   Yellow: We are slightly below our target.
   Red: We are below meeting our target.
   White: We cannot measure our progress.
3. Determine if corrective action needs to be taken.
   How will you adapt the plan to fulfill your mission and vision?

Graphically continuous improvement looks like the following:

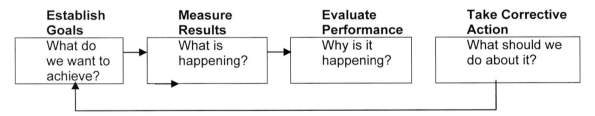

Establish Goals	**Measure Results**	**Evaluate Performance**	**Take Corrective Action**
What do we want to achieve?	What is happening?	Why is it happening?	What should we do about it?

Implementing the Strategic Plan Worksheet

OWNING THE PLAN

Champion Leader:

Accountable to:

Ownership Team:

Key People:

Customer Group:

Customer Group:

Leader:

Leader:

Communicate Plan:

SUPPORTING THE PLAN

People:

Resources:

Structure:

Systems:

Culture:

ADAPTING THE PLAN

Dates:
Meeting dates to
focus on strategy.

Goals:
What do we want to
achieve?

Measure Results:
What is happening?

Evaluate Performance:
Why is it happening?

Take Corrective Action:
What corrective actions
should be taken?

Worksheet: Assessment of Strategic Plan Implementation

Directions: This assessment tool is to be used as a monitoring device. In each area evaluate your company's past efforts **"P"** and current efforts **"C"**. Describe how you will achieve these efforts.

For *example:*

Detailed Action Plan	*None*	_ P_ _ _ _ _ _ _ _ _ _ C_ _ _ _	*Extensive*

Owning the Plan

▪ Detailed Action Plan	None	_ _ _ _ _ _ _ _ _ _ _ _ _ _ _ _	Extensive
▪ Strategic Leader to oversee Strategic Plan	None	_ _ _ _ _ _ _ _ _ _ _ _ _ _ _ _	Champion Leader
▪ Leader or Team for each Customer Group	None	_ _ _ _ _ _ _ _ _ _ _ _ _ _ _ _	Leader/Team
▪ CEO or Top Management Involvement	None	_ _ _ _ _ _ _ _ _ _ _ _ _ _ _ _	High

Supporting the Plan

▪ People - Required Competencies & Skills	Poor	_ _ _ _ _ _ _ _ _ _ _ _ _ _ _ _	Exceptional
▪ Resource Allocation – Personnel, Money, Time	Insufficient	_ _ _ _ _ _ _ _ _ _ _ _ _ _ _ _	Sufficient
▪ Structure	Poor	_ _ _ _ _ _ _ _ _ _ _ _ _ _ _ _	Exceptional
▪ Communication/ Information Operating Systems	None	_ _ _ _ _ _ _ _ _ _ _ _ _ _ _ _	Thorough
▪ Planning System	None	_ _ _ _ _ _ _ _ _ _ _ _ _ _ _ _	Thorough
▪ Compensation – Rewards and Incentives	None	_ _ _ _ _ _ _ _ _ _ _ _ _ _ _ _	Performance Bonus
▪ Corporate Culture	Inconsistent	_ _ _ _ _ _ _ _ _ _ _ _ _ _ _ _	Consistent

Adapting the Plan

▪ Persistence	None	_ _ _ _ _ _ _ _ _ _ _ _ _ _ _ _	Relentless
▪ Scorecard Measured Results	None	_ _ _ _ _ _ _ _ _ _ _ _ _ _ _ _	Extensive
▪ Continuous Improvement	None	_ _ _ _ _ _ _ _ _ _ _ _ _ _ _ _	Ongoing

Adapted from Best, Roger J. Strategies for Growing Customer Value and Profitability, 2000.

104

About M3 Planning

Background
M3 is a strategic planning firm that works with entrepreneurial-spirited organizations. We focus on strategic planning because strategically focused organizations report a 12% increase in performance. We make strategy a reality by organizing your ideas into a practical executionable plan. We do this through assessments, our online planning and execution system, market research, on-site facilitations, and books. We are resource center for everything related to strategy.

M3 stands for *Mission* to *Market* to *Measurement*. Founded in Reno, Nevada in 2000 and based on 15 years of preparatory work, M3 Planning works alongside entrepreneurs to build market-focused organizations. By crystallizing a compelling Mission, assessing the competitive Marketplace, and Measuring the results of its strategies, we help organizations build strategies that are result-oriented. Through an empirically proven process, we give financial meaning to strategy and planning.

Our Services
M3 specializes in working with businesses and organizations that need to better understand their customers and marketplace as a way to drive business. We approach each organization initially by assessing their unique and then working with them to be market-focused in order to unlock their potential for success. We assist them in identifying new opportunities and help them develop new market-focused strategies and organizational plans.

We offer the following content-specific strategic planning systems:

OnStrategyHQ.com
OnStrategyHQ™ will help your business make strategy a competitive advantage. With a complete set of web-based tools, you can easily build, measure, monitor, and revise your strategic plan. Upon completion, you will be provided with a finished plan; a visual strategy map to communicate the plan throughout your organization; and a scorecard to assist in monitoring the plan. This self-guided, online process is recommended for established companies ready to commit time and resources to the planning process.

On-Site Facilitation
Some organizations find that they prefer a more tailored and facilitated approach to developing their strategic plans. To provide a customized strategic planning process, we offer strategic plan development and implementation programs. We work with you and your key staff to facilitate development sessions that result in an optimally-developed strategic plan and implementation programs.

References

Aaker, David A. *Strategic Market Management.* 6th Ed. New York: John Wiley & Sons, Inc., 2001.

Best, Roger J. *Strategies for Growing Customer Value and Profitability*, 2nd Ed. Upper Saddle River: Prentice Hall, 2000.

Biehl, Bobb. *Master-Planning – The Complete Guide for Building a Strategic Plan for Your Business, Church, or Organization.* Nashville: Broadman & Holman Publishers, 1997.

Collins, Jim. *Good to Great.* Harper Business, 2001.

Cook, Kenneth J. *AMA Complete Guide to Strategic Planning for Small Business.* Lincolnwood: NTC Business Books, 1994.

Day, George S. *Market Driven Strategy – Processes for Creating Value.* New York: The Free Press, 1990.

Dobni, Brooke, Dawn Dobni, and George Luffman. "Behavioral Approaches to Marketing Strategy Implementation," *Marketing Intelligence & Planning* 19/6 [2001] 400-408. MCB University Press.

Kaplan, Robert S. and David P. Norton. "Putting the Balanced Scorecard to Work," *Harvard Business Review*, September-October 1993, p.134-147.

Kaplan, Robert S. and David P. Norton. "The Balanced Scorecard-Measures that Drive Performance, " *Harvard Business Review*, January-February 1992, p.71 to 79.

Kaplan, Robert S. and David P. Norton. "Linking the Balanced Scorecard to Strategy," *California Management Review*, Fall v39n1, 1996, p.53 to 79.

Kotler, Philip and Gary Armstrong, *Principles of Marketing*, Tenth Edition. Upper Saddle River, NJ: Pearson/Prentice Hall, 2004.

Lambert, David W. "Towards A Strategy-Balanced Measure Of Business Performance: Conceptualization And Empirical Examination With The Market Orientation Construct," dissertation, Old Dominion University, 2001.

Olsen, Howard W. "Market Orientation: Towards an Understanding in Developing Marketplaces of South America," dissertation, Old Dominion University, 2001. Ann Arbor: UMI, 2002. TX5-538-634, 2001.

Porter, Michael. Competitive Strategy – Techniques for Analyzing Industries and Competitors. New York: The Free Press, 1980.

Slater, Stanley F, Eric M. Olson, Venkateshwar K. Reddy. "Strategy-Based Performance Measurement". *Business Horizons.* July-August 1997, p.37-44).

Thompson, Arthur A., Jr. and A.J. Strickland III. *Strategic Management Concepts and Cases.* Boston: Irwin McGraw-Hill, 1999.

Treacy, Michael and Fred Wiersema, *The Discipline of Market Leaders*. Massachusetts: Addison-Wesley Publishing company, 1995, p.29-43.

VALS Lifestyle Segments, http://www.sric-bi.com/VALS/types.html/, referenced June 16, 2004.

Company:
Plan:

Strategic Plan

Foundation

Our Mission

Our Core Values

Competitive Advantage

What we do best

Organization-wide Strategies

How we will get there

Key Perfomance Indicators

How we measure success

Vision

What our organization looks like

Implementation

How we make strategy a habit